BLACK MIXCELLENCE
A COMPREHENSIVE GUIDE TO BLACK MIXOLOGY

TAMIKA HALL
WITH COLIN ASARE-APPIAH

BLACK MIXCELLENCE

A COMPREHENSIVE GUIDE TO BLACK MIXOLOGY

BLACK MIXCELLENCE

A COMPREHENSIVE GUIDE TO BLACK MIXOLOGY

BY

TAMIKA HALL

WITH

COLIN ASARE-APPIAH

"Is it any wonder that mankind stands open-mouthed before the bartender, considering the mysteries and marvels of an art that borders on magic?"

- The Ideal Bartender, by Tom Bullock

TABLE OF CONTENTS

FOREWORD

Recent research has celebrated some of the Black mixologists, including John Dabney, Tom Bullock, Cato Alexander, and the bartenders from the Black Mixologist Club, just to name a few. While their stories have been lost, Black people have been involved in the mixology industry since Europeans first came to America. Their creativity in cocktails such as the mint julep is legendary, and their contribution to distilling is still evident today in the whiskey and liqueur worlds. In recent times, opportunities are being afforded to Black mixologists to share their stories and to show their craft. Social media, and the public desire to re-create bespoke cocktails that people have enjoyed at bars and now want to make at home, have both been at the forefront of this movement to celebrate Black mixology. This celebration is long overdue, and as a Black mixologist, it's great to see the opportunity, but a lot more work still needs to be done. Diversity only makes the industry stronger. Black mixologists bring a whole cultural pantry of ingredients and flavor profiles to the industry, which can only elevate the community as a whole.

Black Mixcellence delivers recipes from modern-day Black & Brown mixologists, including me (Colin Asare Appiah), Alexis Brown, Barry Johnson, Camille Wilson, Clay Coleman, Dessalyn Pierre, Ed Warner II, Ms Franky Marshall, Glendon Hartley, Ian Burrell, Jaylynn Little, Joe Samuel, Joy Spence, Karl Franz Williams, Kimberly Hunter, Madeline Maldonado, Marlena Richardson, Miguel Soto Rincon, Nigal Vann, Tiffanie Barriere, Douglas Ankrah, and Vance Henderson. These are just some of the Black mixologists who are blazing trails.

Tom Bullock's cocktail book, *The Ideal Bartender*, provides insights into the winter of the last golden age of cocktail culture. The book disappeared as Prohibition swept across the United States and has not been resurrected until recently. It is inspiring that the book was written in the first place, because just a generation earlier, having the ability to read and write could have been a death sentence for an African American. Our history has been oral for a reason, and now we have an opportunity to put our stories in print, and I've always been a strong believer in writing our own histories. Because if we do not write it, others will.

—Colin Asare-Appiah

PROLOGUE

My first conversation about alcohol started in the second grade, when my first Holy Communion class exposed me to the idea that small children could drink wine in church. My parents drank wine at home, and I always wanted to hold a long-stemmed glass and sip, just like they did. I mean, wine was mentioned in the Bible, so it had to be good . . . right? The year of my First Communion was one of the longest years of my life. I had to study the story of the importance of wine to the Catholic religion. Learning the story and prayers was for a greater purpose, though in my mind, it was all so I could receive Communion and sip wine. I distinctly remember my First Communion and taking a giant sip of wine—the priest snatching the chalice away and rolling his eyes as he wiped the spot where my mouth was. I felt so grown up and sat back in my seat with a wine-stained Kool-Aid smile. You're supposed to say prayers after you receive Communion, but as I knelt down on the pew with my eyes tightly shut, all I kept wondering was, "Am I going to be drunk soon?"

Wine and spirits have always had a presence in my life as a woman with Cuban, Jamaican, and Geechee roots. Whether a rub because I was sick or a flavor enhancer in a traditional meal, spirits (particularly rum) played an integral role in my upbringing. My earliest memories of cocktails involved going out to dinner with my parents. For as long as I can remember, my parents always started dinner with cocktails: my mom with an amaretto sour and my dad with an old-fashioned . . . or sometimes a continental, "with Jamaican rum." My dad would pluck the cherry out of my mom's amaretto sour and let me eat it. When I was a kid, the burn of the amaretto was intense, but the nutty almond aftertaste was elite. I looked forward to that moment at every dinner, and as I grew older, I developed my own dinner routine that also began with a cocktail.

At home, Wray & Nephew overproof white rum was a staple item. My aunt, who lived upstairs from me, had a bottle in the kitchen. My parents also had one in the kitchen, and my grandmother kept a bottle nearby at all times. When the bottle was finished, she would use it as storage for her coconut oil. That was one of the weird things I took from her house when she died. That bottle was a symbol of her kitchen,

my family, and all the memories that came with it. She would mix malta con leche condensada when we came over and add Wray & Nephew in it for the adults. She mixed the nonalcoholic version with nothing but ice for the children. I still remember the first time I had the rum version; I was so excited to finally indulge. Nowadays, mixologists have refined the recipe and call that concoction a Malta Fizz. For me, it's still "malta con leche condensada, that drink my grandmother used to make." That drink, that bottle, and those memories help to tell my story. What I didn't know was that the rum and the cocktails were part of a bigger story that continues to unfold as time progresses.

Cocktails and spirits are all part of an industry that we, as African Americans, have played a major role in for years. Service and hospitality are tasks and interactions that African Americans have been providing the United States with for over four hundred years. Some of those tasks and interactions include mixology and the process of creating and serving cocktails. Given the parameters of slavery, service was something we were expected to deliver at all times. Even as such, we did it with a smile and still managed to make a lasting impression. Mixologists/bartenders do a job that requires a variety of skills and a tremendous amount of patience, customer empathy, and enthusiasm.

Like a lot of our contributions to the history of this country, credit wasn't given where credit was due, but the stories and narratives remain. While many of our ancestors couldn't document their journeys and stories as they happened, research allows us to piece together their accomplishments. This book serves as a home for some of our ancestors' stories, contributions, and milestone moments that have greatly affected the mixology industry. BIPOC mixologists and bartenders today are trailblazers, making their mark in the very same industry. In ongoing efforts to preserve the stories of our ancestors from the past. It's only right that we concurrently document and highlight the recipes of some of the people making it happen in the *now*. The stories, libations, and voices of *Black Mixcellence* serve as a testament to the past and as documentation of the present, in the hopes of educating and influencing the future.

THE STORIES

THE GENESIS: POUR OUT A LITTLE FOR THOSE WHO AREN'T HERE

The word "spirits" is synonymous with different types of alcohol. The distillation process, which is how most alcohol is made, is said to have originated in ancient Egypt, where distilling liquids for medicinal purposes involved capturing the "spirit" of the concentrated alcohol through evaporation. This process started to be used more frequently and eventually included the creation of other liquids like alcoholic beverages.

As people started to be taken all over the world due to the slave trade, they took the distillation process with them. Slaves were forced to cultivate, harvest, crush, and sieve sugarcane and to collect the molasses that it created. At some point, the molasses was distilled, and rum was born. Rum became a spirit in high demand among many people. By the 1700s, sugarcane distillation to make rum was one of the primary duties for slaves. Rum was trending with everyone from pirates to servicemen to politicians to royalty. Jamaican rum, specifically, was said to have many health benefits for people who drank it. Rum was the spirit of choice of American colonists, and if it weren't for the labor of slaves, it wouldn't have been available. George Washington distributed over seventy-five gallons of rum and rum punch to voters when he was running for the Virginia House of Burgesses in 1758. Sailors of the British Royal Navy were rationed half a pint of rum a day. Some of the recipes for rum punch floating around included fruit juice, vegetable acid, and vinegar-based shrubs that were rumored to function as health tonics.

Rum became an economic and political pawn as the world began to evolve. To the slaves who made the rum, it became a part of their culture. To date, rum brands like Bacardi, Wray & Nephew, Mountgay Rum, and Appleton Estate are popular and still very important to Latino and Caribbean lifestyles and cultures. Newer brands like Equiano are preserving the story behind the rum and the slave trade that carried it around the world.

Tradition and storytelling have played a huge role in how Black culture has been shared and passed down to generations. Rum and its function among most Caribbean and Latino households is a true testament to that. You know the phrase, "Pour a little out for those who ain't here"? It comes from a tradition that is deeply rooted in African and Caribbean culture. Pouring out a little bit of liquid in honor of the dead dates all the way back to the early days of ancient Egyptian rituals and practices. A translated phrase from the legendary Papyrus of Ani, dating back to the thirteenth century B.C., cites honoring the dead in this passage: "Pour libation for your father and mother who rest in the valley of the dead . . . do not forget to do this even when you are away from home. For as you do for your parents, your children will do for you also . . ."

This tradition was circulated all over the world as slaves continued to move around and incorporate it wherever they were located. It has also been adapted into the history of rum.

Alcoholic spirits weren't the only choice of liquid to be poured: water, milk, honey, and wine were also popular options. Pouring out liquids or libations to honor the dead and nourish the earth is a ritual that has been practiced over time, across a variety of cultures. In Caribbean homes, pouring rum on the floor of a new home is the best way to keep the evil spirits or duppies away. The word *duppy* has African origins and is commonly used to describe ghosts or spirits in most Caribbean countries.

We saw pop culture tap this tradition in the seventies for the movie Cooley High. Writer Eric Monte used the tradition to highlight the death of the character Cochise. His friend Preach poured some out right before he took a sip after his funeral at the cemetery. In 1991, John Singleton had his finger on the pulse of tradition when he wrote Boyz n the Hood. Ice Cube's character, Doughboy, poured out some of his forty to honor all his friends and family who'd been killed. In 1991, the group DRS poured from their forties in the video for their song "Gangsta Lean." A few years later, Tupac Shakur referenced honoring the dead in his song "Pour Out a Little Liquor." Dr. Dre, Juelz Santana, Wu-Tang Clan, and other artists soon followed suit, honoring their homies who were no longer here with either lyrics or video visuals. "Pouring a little out" became more and more popular as time went on and became obligatory within hip-hop culture.

While the culture was shedding light on the tradition, most Caribbean families were using spirits, namely rum, in all aspects of life. In the spirit of keeping tradition, let us start by pouring out a little to honor those who are no longer here and to keep the space free of bad vibes and full of good energy.

THE DARK & STORMY HISTORY OF CARIBBEAN RUM

It is impossible to consider the role of rum in mixology without considering its history, no matter how difficult it might be.

Sugarcane is not an indigenous plant in the Caribbean; it was introduced to the island of Hispaniola by Christopher Columbus. The islands of the Caribbean provided perfect growing conditions for the crop, and by the mid-1600s, most of the major seafaring European countries, including England, France, Spain, Portugal, and the Netherlands, had established sugarcane colonies.

The first recorded mention of rum in the Caribbean is from someone who visited Barbados in 1651. In the 1640s, the English had introduced sugarcane plantations to the island. The English had already been transporting both enslaved people from Africa and convicts to Virginia for decades to work on tobacco plantations, and the introduction of sugarcane in the Caribbean led to a rapid expansion of slavery. Conditions were hard and life was brutal, and enslaved workers had no hope of gaining their freedom, of returning to their former homes, or of seeing an end to their labors.

The elderly and children as young as five were put to work clearing debris from the fields or scaring away birds. Older children and adults planted, tended, and harvested the cane using only basic tools, working through the hours of sunlight; others worked in the sugar mill, which operated day and night in dangerous conditions.

Children of enslaved parents were born into slavery and immediately became the property of the plantation owner. Unfortunately, the hard, physical work meant that many women lost their babies during pregnancy. While this might have been considered a loss for the plantation owner, he knew he could always buy more slaves. Life was cheap.

It was not until 1834, a year after the passage of the Slavery Abolition Act in Britain, that slavery ended in almost all British colonies, including in the Caribbean. This act established a compensation fund of £20,000,000, but this was used to pay the former slave owners rather than those who had suffered as part of the trade.

Even the passage of the act did not make enslaved people completely free immediately. They were required to continue working for their master for a period of up to six years, during which time they were supposed to "learn" how to be free and would be permitted to work for other employers and earn money for themselves. In truth, their situation did not improve significantly.

Slavery was replaced by a form of indentured labor in which workers agreed to work for a fixed period of time without pay as a form of apprenticeship. The men and women who took up these offers of employment came largely from India.

The cultivation of sugarcane for the production of rum has become more mechanized, but the business of rum remains a white-dominated industry. The inability to invest in the islands and the communities that have been a major part of the industry's profitability has meant that few from African American and Caribbean backgrounds are able to climb the ladder of success. While plantation owners were compensated after slavery ended for what were seen as their losses, the same cannot be said for either the enslaved, who went through so much hardship and yet contributed so much to the wealth of those who benefited from their labor, or for their descendants.

There are exceptions, of course. In 1997, Joy Spence of Appleton Estate became the world's first female master blender, and in 2019, Trudiann Branker from Barbados became Mount Gay's first female master blender. Marc Farrell, the founder of Ten To One Rum, is Trinidadian, and Equiano Rum was cofounded by Ian Burrell and named after Olaudah Equiano, a former slave and abolitionist who purchased his own freedom using money he earned by selling rum on the side. There has been a lot of change when it comes to African Americans in the industry. Our presence is strong, and we will continue to make strides and lead the way through.

MEMBERS ONLY:
THE BLACK MIXOLOGISTS CLUB

Black bartenders and mixologists have been doing their thing for quite some time. Cato Alexander, John Dabney, Tom Bullock, and Dick Francis were some of the first Black bartenders to notably plant their feet in the industry. Stories of their successes have been circulating since the late 1700s. It is evident from the early talents of mixologists like Birdie Brown and John Dabney that African Americans had a solid presence in the spirits industry. At that time, most bartenders were white and male.

Slavery and demographics played a huge role in which establishments and social clubs were able to hire Black mixologists. African Americans started gaining their freedom once the Act for the Gradual Abolition of Slavery was initiated in Pennsylvania in the late eighteenth century. One of those people, Cato Alexander, was able to gain his freedom thanks to that act. But before that happened, Alexander had to maneuver through the hardships of slavery. Famous for his Virginia Eggnog and South Carolina Milk Punch, he was a bartender at several bars and inns before opening his own. His mixtures were rumored to be among the first beverages to be called "cocktails," which helped establish mixology as something more than just mixing liquids. He was crowned the Father of Mixology, giving the science of mixing drinks a new level that required talent and creativity.

Alexander was one of the few Black mixologists to open a bar during the slavery era. His tavern, Cato's Bar & Inn, opened in New York City in the late 1700s. Cato's immediately set the standard for bar culture. His tavern focused on quality service and a dope vibe, coupled with top-notch delivery of food and drink. His establishment became a hot spot among white elites, and he was highly regarded by his customers. Cato served the likes of many influential white men of the time, including George Washington. A lot of neighboring white business owners didn't like that and occasionally made things difficult for Alexander. Being a Black business owner in the slavery era, Alexander had frequent violent run-ins with people. Dick Francis is another notable Black mixologist who paved the way for many to follow. Although he was born free in Virginia, he was never taught how to read or write. Francis was behind the bar at a DC hotspot at the time called Hancock's.

Hancock's was a saloon that was known for its cocktails, and Francis was the brains behind their creativity. A bartender at the Senate's restaurant (the Senate had a restaurant at the time), he was highly celebrated for his cocktail creations and service. Hell and Blazes cocktails were a popular option, a drink served in sugar-coated glasses. Francis served the likes of Senator Henry Clay, US Secretary of State Daniel Webster, and other notables who passed through the DC area. Francis is known for his Flowerpot Punch, a daiquiri made with Bank 5 rum and the flavors of rhum agricole (French sugarcane rum), lemon and lime, grenadine, and pineapple syrup.

Even through Prohibition, Black mixologists flourished and continued to stay in the mix, literally. It was important for these men to excel at their jobs so they could make notable names for themselves for future opportunities. Their reputations preceded them, and people of importance came looking for men like Dabney, Cato, Bullock, and Francis by name to enjoy their spirits. As the twentieth century approached and more African American mixologists and bartenders started to emerge, there was a need for a safe professional haven for Black and Brown bartenders.

The Black Mixologists Club, founded by R. R. Bowie and J. Burke Edelin in 1898, was the perfect professional space for Black bartenders/mixologists to gather and network . . . and have some of the best parties. The club became an elite but popular group in the DC area. Having a place for Black bartenders to congregate was important to both their success and camaraderie as their popularity and demand in the industry increased. The existence of an organization like the Black Mixologists Club meant that current mixologists and up-and-coming mixologists had a place to meet, exchange ideas, and discuss potential opportunities. As more and more African Americans gained their freedom, rules of segregation initiated the need for more Black communities and businesses, especially in the DC area. The increase in Black-owned bars and restaurants saw a need for more mixologists and bartenders. Sharing stories and words of support and encouragement has always been a welcome part of the mixology industry. The Black Mixologists Club helped to keep that as an active part of the organization to help motivate those in the industry.

Uncle Nearest
Always Bet On Black, Jack

African American slaves provided service to the United States from as early as 1618. Bartending/mixology fell under that umbrella of services. Slaves learned to cook, clean, and perform a variety of duties that eventually translated into hospitality jobs and careers. These jobs helped them make money to eventually buy their freedom and establish careers for themselves once slavery ended. Documentation of the African American experience and proof of their services have both been lost in translation for a variety of reasons. The further back in time you go, the less information is available. As a result of constant research and data collection, however, quite a few narratives have started to surface. One of those narratives is the story of Nathan Green, better known as Uncle Nearest (or Nearis).

Born in 1820, Green was one of the top whiskey distillers in Lynchburg, Tennessee. Green was a slave on Reverend Dan Call's farm, where he once operated the distillery. The distillery was located behind the house of Reverend Call, and for years, people thought that's who was operating the distillery. While the reverend wasn't the distiller, the townspeople gave him a lot of grief because a man of the church shouldn't have been involved in such operations. Eventually, the reverend passed the distillery to a friend, and Green continued to make whiskey there.

Green's whiskey distillation involved a charcoal water-filtering process that he had adapted from West Africa. The charcoal was made from sugar maples and played an important role in filtering water. Uncle Nearest found a way to filter whiskey through this same charcoal process. This filtration procedure would become known as the Lincoln County Process and is still among the most innovative methods of distillation to date. This process is what separated Kentucky bourbon from Tennessee whiskey. Green was the brains behind the whiskey-distillation process and the famous recipe that gave the Jack Daniel's brand its legs. In 1856, a young man named Jasper Daniel came to the farm looking for work and was intrigued by what Green was doing. The townspeople spoke highly of Green's whiskey and its smooth flavor. Daniel became a student of Green's and learned all about the distillation process.

A few years later, Daniel's entrepreneurial spirit had kicked in, and he was selling Green's whiskey all over town.

In 1865, when the Thirteenth Amendment passed, Green was officially a free man. Soon after, Daniel bought the distillery and named it after himself: not Jasper Daniel but Jack Daniel. The locals called him "Uncle Jack," and he preferred that name over Jasper. Green continued to work at the Jack Daniel's distillery as the master distiller, the first African American documented to hold that title. Daniel and Green made whiskey together for quite some time. In 1884, Green retired his position and put his final batch of whiskey to barrel. Jasper Daniel had the distillation process down to a science by that point and continued to make whiskey and grow the Jack Daniel's brand into what it is today.

In 2017, Fawn Weaver decided that she was going to give Nathan Green the representation he deserved. She launched the Uncle Nearest Premium Whiskey brand. A new distillery is now run by the descendants of their ancestor, Nathan Green. The distillery is located down the road from the farm where Green used to work. The story of Uncle Nearest was hearsay in Lynchburg for quite some time. It wasn't until countless hours of research had been conducted and the discovery of a trove of documents that the story of Uncle Nearest could be pieced together.

Good Hooch Hits Different
Bertie "Birdie" Brown

On January 17, 1920, the Eighteenth Amendment delivered a constitutional ban on the sale and production of alcoholic beverages that rocked the spirits industry. This ban initiated Prohibition, which put a screeching halt to the importation, transportation, and consumption of alcoholic beverages that lasted until 1933. Imagine a world without access to alcohol or being able to hang out with your friends at the bar and have a cocktail. Bars and saloons were forced to close, and people had to find other ways to gather and have cocktails. Not only were patrons inconvenienced, but bartenders/mixologists had to find alternate means to support themselves. People had no idea how long Prohibition would last and decided to not sit around and wait for it to end. They started to think about other ways to make money . . . and alcohol.

Secret bars and saloons known as speakeasies started popping up shortly after Prohibition began. They were well-disguised establishments that were meant to replace the public-facing bars and saloons that had been closed. A password was often required for entry and sometimes even an invite. Speakeasies served all kinds of beverages, including hoochinoo, nicknamed hooch, a low-grade whiskey that was distilled and produced illegally. Since whiskey wasn't legally allowed to be sold, speakeasies depended on hooch sales to make money. People soon figured out ways to produce their own hooch for retail sales. One of those people was Bertie "Birdie" Brown.

Brown was an African American woman who traveled from Missouri to Montana to make a new life for herself in the early 1900s. She belonged to a small population of African American women who decided to homestead in Montana. Her homestead was located in Fergus County, where she quickly developed a solid reputation along Brickyard Creek. She was known to offer people who were traveling a hot meal and a "home away from home" while they were passing through. Brown was single and lived alone with her cat. Farming and bootlegging became primary sources of income at that time. During Prohibition, her parlor was rumored to produce the best hooch in the country. Everyone was trying to produce their own stash, so it was important to be good at it. She had her process and recipe down pat, and her hooch was in high demand. Not only was her hooch

smooth, but the warmth and hospitality of her parlor drew people from near and far. She quickly carved out a name for herself, and her hooch business flourished during Prohibition. She still produced plenty of hooch despite the warnings from the revenue officers who would visit her parlor often to warn her to stop brewing.

As it happened, Brown was a multitasker who managed to do a few things at once. Homesteading, producing hooch, and doing household chores added up to a lot of work for one person. One day, she was using gasoline to steam garments while tending to her hooch batch, and the still exploded in her face. The burns from the explosion were so intense that she died a few hours later, leaving a legacy of top-notch hooch making behind. Brown died in 1933, the same year that Prohibition ended. She never got to see its end, but her hooch work was widely known and is still creating a buzz to this day. Who knows what success Brown might have had once the ban was lifted? Both her cabin and her legacy — and a brand of hooch named in her honor, Birdie Brown Plain Hooch — stand tall today and will continue to hold a place in mixology history.

OFF TO THE RACES: THE MINT JULEP

When people think of the Kentucky Derby, they often think of the Garland of Roses, the Winner's Circle, the Hat Parade, and, of course, the mint julep cocktail. The mint julep, a bourbon-based cocktail, is the signature drink of the Kentucky Derby Festival and is served throughout the entire event. The history of the mint julep runs deep, with stories about its existence starting as early as the 1700s. The mint julep began as a concoction mixed with camphor that was meant to cure stomach ailments and other digestive issues. As time progressed, the recipe was refined, the ingredients changed, and it evolved into a popular cocktail. The mint julep had a whole life between the 1700s and the 1930s, when it was introduced as the signature drink of the Derby. It was Black mixologists who gave it the push it needed to become popular.

During the nineteenth century, the mint julep was on heavy rotation in the South. John Dabney, Jasper Crouch, and Jim Cook were the three Black mixologists who gave the mint julep its swag. Crouch, who identified himself as a free person of color, is known to have been the catalyst for the mint julep's popularity in Virginia. He called himself a caterer, which was a person who specialized in making and serving both food and drink. Crouch worked at the Buchanan Spring Quoit Club and the Richmond Light Infantry Blues, two prestigious clubs in Richmond. Not only was he known for his cooking skills, but his cocktails were also on point. His Ice Punch was a hit at both clubs. The punch recipe included Jamaican rum, French brandy, and a little bit of Murdock Madeira, a popular cocktail ingredient during the nineteenth century. Madeira is a fortified Portuguese wine that was used in many cooking recipes as well. He was also known for making classic mint juleps, which he served exclusively at the Quoit Club.

John Dabney also played an important role in making the mint julep recipe pop, to quickly become a must-have in every bar. Born a slave, he got his mixologist experience while working for his owner, Cora Williamson DeJarnette, who owned a hotel in Richmond where she let Dabney work for a time. She made sure he had the proper training in bartending and culinary skills. He got most of his experience in both there and served his famed mint julep to many. The julep wasn't his only claim to food and drink fame: his terrapin stew and canvasback duck were the talk of the town. After a while, Dabney left his job at the hotel and started working independently. He made his own money, but he still had to give a portion to DeJarnette for payment.

As time went on, Dabney moved around and began working at the Ballard House Hotel. He teamed up with another Black mixologist named Jim Cook, and the two dubbed the Great Julep Makers of the South. Their mint juleps got rave reviews, and people came from all over for their julep experience. Edward, Prince of Wales (before he became King Edward VII), was said to have been served a mint julep à la Dabney during one of his diplomatic visits to Virginia. He made it a point to go to the Ballard House to have a julep. He evidently intended to have one and ended up having several. He was so impressed that he decided to return the next day for two more, just moments before his trip back home.

Prince Edward wasn't the only high-profile figure to be impressed by Dabney's juleps. Charles Dickens came to Virginia and dragged everything but the julep. Dabney's recipe was simple yet potent, and his presentation was impressive. The tall ice in the silver cup was accompanied by a robust array of fruits for garnish.

Dabney bought freedom for himself and his wife once the Civil War ended. He continued to keep bars at some of Richmond's most prominent food and drink locations. His ability to network and maintain relationships with people he'd met years prior gave him a huge advantage once he became a free man. The mint julep was dubbed the signature cocktail of the Kentucky Derby in 1938. It continues to play a major role in the events of the Derby and is still served in bars and restaurants around the world.

INGREDIENTS
AND TECHNIQUES

SIMPLE SYRUP

Room-temperature water
Granulated sugar

Combine equal parts water to sugar in a pan over low heat. Stir until sugar has dissolved, and stir some more. Let cool to room temperature, then refrigerate for 2 hours. The final syrup mixture can be stored in the refrigerator in an airtight container.

EXPRESS

Hold the citrus peel between your thumb and forefinger. Twist over the glass, peel side down, to express the oil onto the top of the cocktail.

BOSTON SHAKER SET

This is the preferred shaker set for higher volumes of liquids.

SMOKE TRAILS (FOR GARNISH)

Use a culinary torch to lightly char the tip of the sprigs so that there's a smoke trail.

SHAKE AND STRAIN

Fill the glass with ice and water and let it sit. Fill a 16-ounce Boston shaker one-third full with ice. Fill a 28-ounce Boston shaker with the ingredients. Fit the smaller shaker into the larger shaker and vigorously shake for 7 seconds. Empty the glass of the ice and water and filter the shaken ingredients into the chilled glass.

TOPPPING OFF

Finish a cocktail with a user-determined amount of an ingredient, such as club soda or cava.

WHISK(E)Y

CHAI OLD-FASHIONED

"Bartender Barry" Johnson

GLASSWARE
Old-fashioned

GARNISH
Cinnamon stick

ICE
Large cubes

INGREDIENTS
- 2 ounces Uncle Nearest 1856
- ¼ ounce Chai Tea Syrup (see below)
- 1 dash Angostura Aromatic Bitters
- 5–10 drops Bob's Vanilla Bitters

METHOD
Add all ingredients to a mixing glass. Add ice and stir for 30 revolutions. Strain in an old-fashioned glass with a large ice cube. Garnish with a cinnamon stick.

SPECIAL INGREDIENTS

Chai Tea Syrup: **2 chai tea bags • 1½ cup brown sugar**

Add 8 ounces of hot water to the tea bags and let tea steep for 10 minutes. Remove the tea bags and add tea to a small saucepan with the brown sugar. Bring to a low boil and let simmer for 10 minutes. Remove from heat and let cool completely before use.

BASIL JOE-JITO

Camille Wilson

GLASSWARE
Large rocks

GARNISH
Basil
Lemon

ICE
Cubes

INGREDIENTS
- 4 blackberries
- 2–4 basil leaves
- 1 ounce honey
- 1 ounce lemon juice
- 2 ounces Whiskey

METHOD
Muddle berries, basil leaves, and honey in a cocktail shaker. Add lemon juice, whiskey, and ice. Shake until chilled. Pour into an ice-filled glass and serve. Using a stainless-steel cocktail pick, garnish with a slice of lemon and 2 basil leaves.

SPECIAL INGREDIENTS

Liquid Gold: Warm water • Honey

In a bowl, mix ½ ounce warm water with ½ ounce honey. Stir until the honey is dissolved, then set aside.

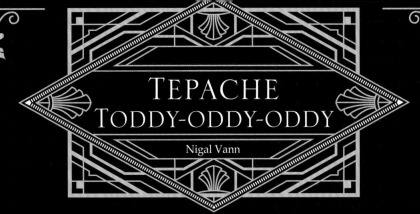

TEPACHE
TODDY-ODDY-ODDY

Nigal Vann

GLASSWARE
Mug

GARNISH
Lemon slice

ICE
None

INGREDIENTS
- 1 ½ oz Glenlivet 12 yr Whiskey
- ½ oz chamomile infused orange liqueur (see below)
- ½ oz lemon juice
- ¾ oz tepache syrup (see below)
- 5 drops of allspice dram
- 5 drops of BBQ bitters
- Hot water

METHOD
Build in a mug, add hot water.

SPECIAL INGREDIENTS

Tepache Syrup: 366g pineapple chunks • 50g pineapple juice • 170g maple syrup
120g brown sugar • 8g cinnamon sticks • 200g water

Put all ingredients on simmer, low heat for 15 mins. Add 2oz of Glenlivet 12.

Chamomile Infused Orange Liqueur: 8oz orange liqueur • 24g of chamomile tea

Infuse for at least 1 hour.

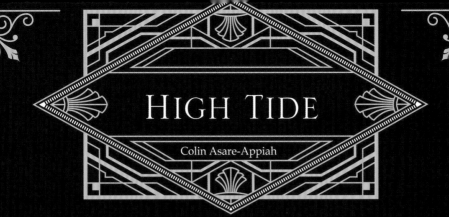

HIGH TIDE

Colin Asare-Appiah

GLASSWARE
Julep

GARNISH
4 mint sprigs
Baby's breath

ICE
Crushed

INGREDIENTS
- 2 ounces Bacardi Superior Rum
- 1 ounce Kleos Mastiha liqueur
- 2 ounces honeydew melon, sliced
- Pinch of Himalayan pink salt
- Pinch of cracked black pepper

METHOD
Gently muddle the mint in a cocktail tin. Add all other ingredients. Shake and strain over crushed ice, add garnish, and serve.

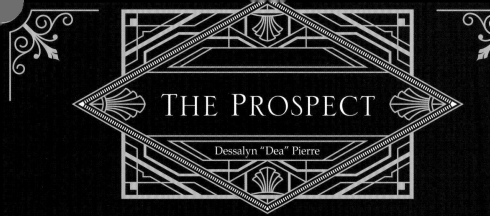

THE PROSPECT

Dessalyn "Dea" Pierre

GLASSWARE
Collins

GARNISH
Lime wheel

ICE
Cubes

INGREDIENTS
- 3 ounces Homemade Sorrel (see below)
- 1 ounce Honey sage syrup (see below)
- 2 dashes orange bitters
- 1 ¾ ounces Maker's Mark Bourbon

METHOD
Build the sorrel, honey sage syrup, orange bitters, and bourbon in a Collins glass filled ⅓ with cubed ice. Lightly stir the partially filled glass with a bar spoon to ensure the ingredients are properly mixed. Garnish and serve.

SPECIAL INGREDIENTS

Homemade Sorrel: 6 cups of water • 5 cloves • 5 allspice • 2 star of anise or ½ teaspoon anise seeds
1 cup hibiscus (tea leaves) • ½ cup raw sugar (any sugar can substitute)

Boil 6 cups of water and add cloves, all spice, anise, and ginger for about 3-4 minutes on medium heat. Lower heat and add hibiscus and sugar. Stir for two minutes, turn off heat, and let cool to room temperature.

Honey Sage Syrup: 1 cup of water • ½ cup honey • 10 sage leaves

In a saucepan on medium high heat, boil all ingredients for 2-3 minutes. Occasionally stirring. Turn off heat and allow syrup to cool off.

FESTIVAL AT THE LAKE COCKTAIL

Clay "The Bartender" Coleman

GLASSWARE
Collins

GARNISH
Bamboo stick
Basil sprig
3 thinly sliced peach slices

ICE
Crushed

INGREDIENTS
- ½ ounce fresh lemon juice
- 1 ounce Uncle Waithley's Ginger Beer
- 1½ ounces spiced tea, steeped for 20 mins. and cooled
- 1½ ounces peach-basil syrup (see below)
- 1½ ounces red Fresno pepper–infused Maker's Mark (see below)
- 2 dashes Angostura bitters

METHOD
Build the drink in the order above in a Collins glass filled ⅓ with crushed ice. Lightly stir the partially filled glass with a bar spoon to ensure the liquid contents are properly mixed. Top the drink off with more crushed ice. Cover the fresh crushed ice with more Angostura bitters on top. Garnish with three thinly sliced peach slices layered on top of one another and skewered on a bamboo stick. The peaches should form a mini "stairway" resting on the rim of the glass. Add a fresh sprig of basil, lightly slapping the sprig first to release the aroma. Add a reusable or compostable straw to the drink and enjoy!

SPECIAL INGREDIENTS

Peach-Basil Syrup: Peach, sliced • 1 cup white cane sugar • ¼ ounce liquid honey • 12 basil leaves ¼ ounce apple cider vinegar

Thinly slice 1 peach into 16 slices and place it in a big, deep bowl with an equal ratio of organic white cane sugar. Add ¼ ounce liquid honey and carefully mix everything without breaking apart the peach slices. Make sure every inch of every slice is completely covered in sugar. Let this mixture sit in the bowl for 5 hours, lightly stirring the peaches once an hour to keep the slices covered in sugar. Lightly muddle the basil leaves inside a mason jar to release the oils and aromatics in the leaves. Carefully pour all the contents of the bowl into the mason jar with the muddled basil. Close the jar and lightly shake the jar for 2 minutes, or until the basil leaves are completely soggy. Taste to ensure that the syrup now has notes of basil. Pour the completed syrup through a fine-mesh strainer and squeeze the remaining soaked produce through a cheesecloth to get out the remaining liquid. Add ¼ ounce apple cider vinegar to the syrup. Keep refrigerated and make sure you always shake it properly before pouring.

Red Fresno Pepper–Infused Maker's Mark:

Thinly slice and deseed 2 red Fresno peppers and place them in a mason jar. Lightly muddle the sliced peppers and pour 17 ounces of Maker's Mark into the mason jar. Vigorously shake the mason jar for 1 minute. Allow the infusion to sit for 2 hours, shaking vigorously again every half hour. Strain liquid through a fine-mesh strainer and squeeze the remaining soaked peppers through a cheesecloth to get out the remaining liquid, then discard the Fresno peppers. The infusion is now complete. Keep refrigerated and make sure you always shake it properly before pouring.

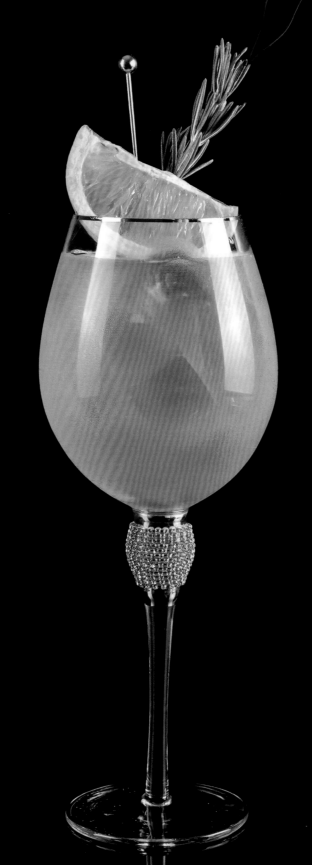

Up All Night

Clay "The Bartender" Coleman

Glassware
Chilled red wine glass

Garnish
Grapefruit wedge
Cocktail skewer

Ice
Cubes

Ingredients
- 5 ounces Rosemary Sage Simple Syrup (see below)
- 1 ounce fresh red grapefruit juice
- ½ ounce Saint George Bruto Americano
- 1½ ounce Maker's Mark 46
- 1 grapefruit
- 3 rosemary sprigs
- 3 sage sprigs
- 7 ounces water
- 1 cup organic white sugar

Method
Put the cubed ice in the chilled wine glass. Build the Rosemary Sage Simple Syrup, grapefruit juice, Saint George Bruto Americano, and Maker's Mark 46 in the chilled wine glass and lightly stir with a barspoon. Cut a grapefruit wedge (an eighth of a whole grapefruit) and skewer it with a cocktail skewer for garnish. Position the wedge on top of the drink to where it looks like a half-moon in the sky. Place a sprig of fresh rosemary into the glass and have it leaning toward the opposite direction of the wedge, creating a V shape.

Optional: Using a culinary torch, lightly char the tip of the sprig so that there's a smoke trail coming off the rosemary.

Special Ingredients

Rosemary Sage Simple Syrup: 3 sprigs rosemary (evenly sized) • 3 sprigs sage (evenly sized)

Place the rosemary and sage in the metal tin of a Boston shaker set. The ratio of sage to rosemary should be even. Next, lightly muddle the herbs inside the tin to release the oils. After muddling, carefully pour the boiling water into the tin. Make sure all the herbs are fully submerged. Let the herbs steep and sit in the water for 30 minutes. Next, strain and separate the herbs from the water by pouring the liquid through a fine-mesh strainer. Be sure to squeeze all the excess liquid from the herbs before discarding them. At this point, you'll need to remeasure your herbal water to find out exactly how much liquid you have. Once you know the exact amount of liquid, you'll then add an equal amount of organic white cane sugar to the liquid. This is to factor in any water that evaporates as the herbs steep. The goal is to create a 1 to 1 ratio of sugar to herbal water. Thoroughly stir the mixture until all the sugar crystals have completely dissolved. Finally, transfer your completed syrup into a storage bottle.

ON A BEACH SOMEWHERE

Marlena "Miko" Richardson

GLASSWARE
Chilled hurricane

GARNISH
Maraschino cherry
Pineapple wedge

ICE
Large cubes

INGREDIENTS
- 2 ounces Maker's Mark 46
- 1 ounce Lychee Syrup (see below)
- Juice of 1 lime
- ½ ounce maraschino cherry liqueur
- 3 ounce cranberry juice
- 3 ounces pineapple juice

METHOD
Pour all ingredients into a shaker with ice and shake vigorously. Pour the mixture into a chilled hurricane glass, garnish with maraschino cherries and a pineapple wedge, and serve.

SPECIAL INGREDIENTS

Lychee Syrup: 6-8 lychees

Peel the lychees. Remove the large seed from center and cut into pieces. Add the pieces to a small saucepan with 1 cup of sugar and ¾ cup of water and bring to a boil, then simmer for 10 minutes or until the fruit is tender. Allow to cool and strain into a squeeze bottle.

HOT STONE MASSAGE

Marlena "Miko" Richardson

GLASSWARE
Highball

GARNISH
Cucumber Ribbons (see below)
Red jalapeño slices

ICE
Cubes

INGREDIENTS
- 2 ounces Cucumber Purée (see below)
- ½ ounce Lychee Syrup (see below)
- 1½ ounce Maker's Mark
- Lemon-lime soda to top

METHOD
Pour all ingredients into a shaker with ice and shake vigorously. Pour the mixture into a chilled hurricane glass, garnish with maraschino cherries and a pineapple wedge, and serve.

SPECIAL INGREDIENTS

Cucumber Purée: 1 large or 2 small cucumbers

Peel the cucumbers and cut into smaller pieces. Place pieces in a blender and puree until smooth. Strain into a bowl through a mesh sieve to remove seeds and larger pieces. Pour the puree into a squeeze bottle and set aside.

Lychee Syrup: 6–8 lychees • 1 cup sugar • ¾ cup of water

Peel lychees, remove the large seed from the centers, and cut into pieces. Add the pieces to a small saucepan with the sugar and water and bring to a boil. Simmer for 10 minutes or until the fruit is tender. Allow to cool and then strain into a squeeze bottle.

Cucumber Ribbons:

Take a freshly washed cucumber and, using a vegetable peeler, peel 2–3 strips lengthwise that feature the skin and cucumber "meat." Don't use the very first strip, which would be mostly skin. Fill the highball glass about ⅓ full with ice and place 1 ribbon along the inside of the glass and finish filling the glass with ice. The other cucumber slice will be ribboned and held in place with a cocktail sword.

Red Jalapeño Slices:

For the cocktail, use a ripe, green jalapeño and cut into rings. For the garnish, use a red jalapeño cut into rings at an angle for the top of the cocktail sword before adding the cucumber ribbon with another slice.

DUC DE BOURBON

Ms Franky Marshall

GLASSWARE
Chilled coupe

GARNISH
Roasted Pumpkin Seed Oil (see below)

ICE
None

INGREDIENTS
- ¼ ounce pear liqueur
- ½ ounce maraschino liqueur
- 1 ounce Bourbon
- 1 ounce Pommeau de Normandie

METHOD
Add all ingredients to a mixing glass and stir with ice until cold. Strain into a small cocktail glass, garnish, and serve.

SPECIAL INGREDIENTS

Roasted Pumpkin Seed Oil:

Using a small brush, "paint" oil horizontally onto one side of glass just under the lip. Then add 3 drops of oil on top of the cocktail.

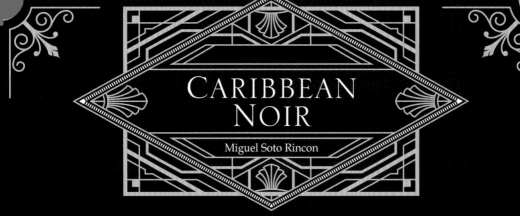

CARIBBEAN NOIR

Miguel Soto Rincon

GLASSWARE
Georgian punch

GARNISH
Lemon peel
Banana leaf

ICE
Large cubes

INGREDIENTS
- 1½ ounce Maker's Mark Bourbon
- 1 ounce rooibos organic red tea
- 8 ounces Pedro Ximénez Jerez sherry
- 2 dashes Coffee and Coconut Extract-Infused Aromatic Bitters (see below)
- 2 ounces organic coconut extract

METHOD
Build all the ingredients in a Georgian punch glass with a large ice cube. Gently stir the liquid with a barspoon.

SPECIAL INGREDIENTS

Coffee and Coconut Extract–Infused Aromatic Bitters: 6 ounces medium-body coffee beans
8 ounces aromatic bitters • 2 ounces organic coconut extract

Place coffee beans inside a 10-ounce mason jar, then add aromatic bitters and organic coconut extract. Seal the jar and shake it really hard. Let it sit for 24 hours, shaking the mixture a few times during that period. Then, to infuse the Pedro Ximénez (PX), use 8 ounces of PX and 2½ tablespoons of the red tea. Heat the PX with the loose-leaf tea for 5 minutes on medium-low heat. Allow it to cool. Place the infusion in the refrigerator for 1 hour. Double-strain the mixture. Add 1 teaspoon of active charcoal to the mixture, shake it, and bottle it.

BUN BE SOMEONE

Ed Warner II

GLASSWARE
Double rocks

GARNISH
Cinnamon smoke

ICE
Large cubes

INGREDIENTS
• 2 ounces Maker's Mark
• 1 ounce Vanilla Cinnamon Simple Syrup (see below)
• ½ ounce Licor 43
• ½ ounce Italicus
• 2–3 barspoons Pedro Ximénez Jerez sherry

METHOD
Pour all ingredients into a cocktail tin. Stir and strain over a large ice cube. If you have access to a smoke bubble gun (if not, a regular smoke gun will do), prep it with the cinnamon chips. Combine all ingredients in a mixing glass with ice and stir rigorously for 30 seconds.

Bubble finish (preferred): In a double rocks glass with a large clear cube or chunk of ice, strain the cocktail and top with a golf ball–size bubble of cinnamon smoke.

No-bubble finish: Complete with a thin layer of cinnamon smoke.

SPECIAL INGREDIENTS

Vanilla Cinnamon Simple Syrup: **2–3 medium cinnamon sticks • 1 cup water • 1 cup demerara sugar**
3 Madagascar bourbon vanilla beans

In a saucepan, add water and cinnamon sticks and bring to a rolling boil for about 2 minutes; then add the sugar and stir until it dissolves. Turn the heat down to a simmer and split and scrape the vanilla beans. Add both pods and beans to the syrup and simmer covered for 20 minutes. Remove from heat and let steep for another 30 minutes.

PRALINE PRINCE

"Bartender Barry" Johnson

GLASSWARE
Coupe

GARNISH
Coconut flakes

ICE
Cubes

INGREDIENTS
• 1 ounce Uncle Nearest 1856
• 1 ounce condensed milk
• 1 ounce Coconut Praline Syrup (see right and below)

METHOD
Prepare the Coconut Praline Syrup. Let syrup cool completely before use. Add all the ingredients to a cocktail shaker. Dry-shake without ice for 30 seconds. Add ice to shaker and shake for 15 to 20 seconds or until shaker is frosty on the outside. Double-strain into a coupe glass with a Hawthorne strainer and a fine-mesh strainer. Serve.

SPECIAL INGREDIENTS

Coconut Praline Syrup: **1 cup brown sugar**
1 cup coconut water • 1 cup crushed pecans

Combine brown sugar and coconut water in a small saucepan. Turn heat on medium and stir until sugar has dissolved. Add the crushed pecans. Once the mixture reaches a boil, reduce heat and let simmer on low for 15 minutes. Remove from heat, let cool completely, and transfer to a clean glass container.

HYE SUNSET

Ed Warner II

GLASSWARE
Rocks

GARNISH
None

ICE
Large cubes

INGREDIENTS
- 1½ ounces Garrison Brothers Small Batch Bourbon
- ¼ ounce amaretto liqueur
- ¼ ounce Combier Crème de Pêche de Vigne liqueur
- ¼ ounce Bénédictine herbal liqueur
- Splash of Héritages Côtes du Rhône
- ¾ ounce lemon juice
- ¾ ounce Rosemary Syrup (see right)

METHOD
Combine ingredients (with the exception of the wine) in a shaker with ice and shake vigorously for approximately 15 seconds. Double-strain into a rocks glass with ice and carefully float approximately ¼ ounce of the wine over the cocktail.

SPECIAL INGREDIENTS

Rosemary Syrup: 1 cup room-temperature water 1 cup granulated sugar • ¼ cup of rosemary leaves

Combine the water, sugar, and rosemary leaves in a pan over low heat. Stir until sugar has dissolved, then stir some more. Remove the mixture from the heat and let steep for half an hour. Let cool to room temperature, then strain the syrup into a sterilized glass jar and refrigerate.

JUST CHILL

Kimberly Hunter

GLASSWARE
Lowball

GARNISH
Orange peel
Edible flower

ICE
Cubes

INGREDIENTS
- 2 ounces rye Whiskey
- 1 chamomile tea bag
- ½ ounce Liquid Gold (see right)
- 2–3 dashes Angostura bitters
- Orange peel

METHOD
Pour the whiskey into a mixing glass. Steep the chamomile tea bag in the whiskey for about 7 minutes. While that's steeping, make the Liquid Gold. Go back to the whiskey and tea infusion and remove the tea bag. Add in the Liquid Gold and bitters and stir for about 10 seconds. Add ice to the lowball glass. Strain the cocktail over the ice. Take the orange peel and express it over the cocktail. Drop the orange peel into the glass with an edible flower and serve.

SPECIAL INGREDIENTS

Liquid Gold: Warm water • Honey

In a bowl, mix ½ ounce warm water with ½ ounce honey. Stir until the honey is dissolved, then set aside.

MASON

Colin Asare-Appiah

GLASSWARE
Large rocks

GARNISH
Lemon twist

ICE
Cubes

INGREDIENTS
- 2 ounces Dewar's 12 Year Old Whisky
- 1 ounce St Germain Elderflower Liqueur
- 2 ounces blackberry purée (see right)
- ½ ounce fresh lemon juice

METHOD
Shake all ingredients over ice. Strain into an ice-filled rocks glass, garnish, and serve.

SPECIAL INGREDIENTS

Blackberry Purée: 1 pint blackberries
Place the pint of berries in a food processor and process until pureed. Using a mesh strainer, strain the mixture over a bowl; discard any particles. Store in an airtight Mason jar and keep refrigerated until ready to use.

TEQUILA/
MEZCAL

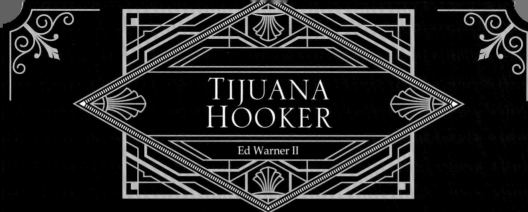

TIJUANA HOOKER

Ed Warner II

GLASSWARE
Double rocks

GARNISH
Beer on the side

ICE
Cubes

INGREDIENTS
- 2 ounces Don Julio Reposado Tequila
- 1 ounce fresh lime juice
- 1 ounce pineapple juice
- ½ ounce Chinola passion fruit liqueur
- ½ ounce Licor 43
- 1 ounce Madagascar Vanilla Simple Syrup (see below)
- 3 ounces side of light-bodied beer

METHOD
Combine ingredients in a shaker and shake vigorously for 10 seconds. Strain over ice in a double rocks glass and serve with a side of beer.

SPECIAL INGREDIENTS

Madagascar Vanilla Simple Syrup: 1 vanilla pod • 1 cup white sugar • 1 cup water

Slice the vanilla bean lengthwise (so it opens like a book) and place it in a ziplock bag with the sugar. Seal the bag and shake vigorously for 3 minutes. Let the mixture rest for at least an hour. Add the water to a saucepan and bring to a low boil. Add the sugar and turn down the heat. Stir until almost clear. Cover and simmer for an hour. Let cool, then pour the syrup into a sterilized glass jar.

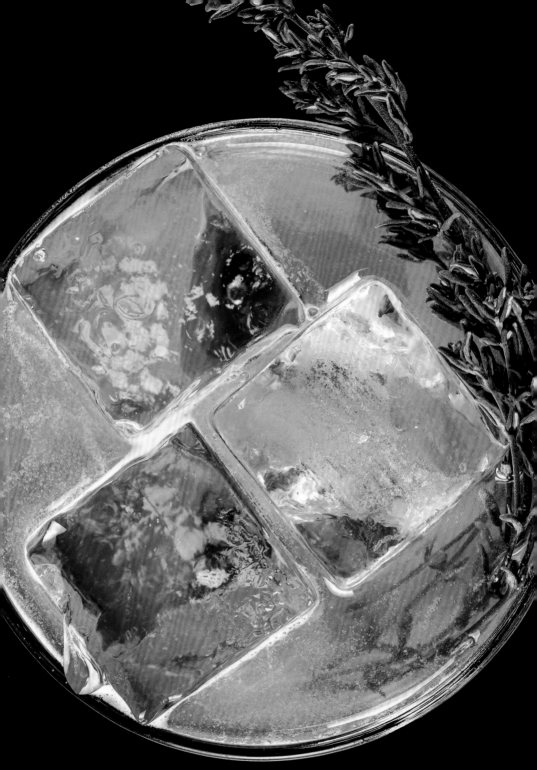

ARRIVAL THYME

Tiffanie Barriere

GLASSWARE
Rocks

GARNISH
3 thyme sprig

ICE
Cubes

INGREDIENTS
- 2 ounces Don Julio Reposado Tequila
- ½ ounce agave
- ½ ounce fresh lime juice
- ½ ounce Campari

METHOD
Combine all ingredients in a cocktail shaker with ice and shake cold. Double-strain into a rocks glass with fresh ice. Garnish with fresh thyme sprigs and serve.

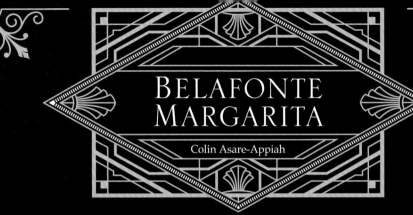

BELAFONTE MARGARITA

Colin Asare-Appiah

GLASSWARE
Margarita

GARNISH
Piece of watermelon

ICE
Cubes

INGREDIENTS
- 1 ounce Ilegal Mezcal Joven
- 1 ounce Martini Fiero
- ½ ounce fresh lime juice
- 2 ounces fresh watermelon (blend pieces)
- 3 slices habanero peppers
- ½ ounce Simple Syrup (see pg. 14)

METHOD
Lightly muddle the peppers in a cocktail tin. Add all the other ingredients. Shake and fine-strain into a chilled margarita glass, garnish, and serve.

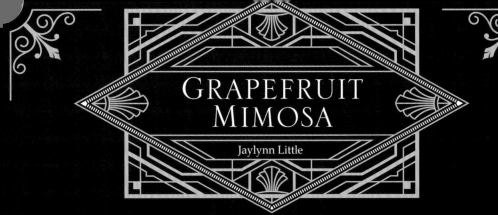

GRAPEFRUIT MIMOSA

Jaylynn Little

GLASSWARE
Champagne flute

GARNISH
1 sprig rosemary

ICE
None

INGREDIENTS
• 1½ ounce Tequila
• 2 ounces Grapefruit Simple Syrup (see below)
• Cava, chilled

METHOD
Pour the tequila and Grapefruit Simple Syrup into a champagne flute and top off with the cava. Garnish with the rosemary and serve.

SPECIAL INGREDIENTS

Grapefruit Simple Syrup: 2 slices of grapefruit peel • 1 cup fresh grapefruit juice • 1 cup sugar
2 grapefruit wedges

Add all the ingredients to a small pot and stir until the sugar has dissolved. Bring to a boil, then reduce the heat to low and let it simmer for 10–15 minutes. Remove from the heat and store in a glass jar in the refrigerator.

OCHA

Colin Asare-Appiah

GLASSWARE
Rocks

GARNISH
Shaved radish

ICE
Cubes

INGREDIENTS
- 1 ounce Tequila Cazadores Blanco
- 1 ounce Ilegal Mezcal Joven
- 1 ounce Agave
- 3 ounces beet juice
- ½ ounce fresh lime juice
- ½ ounce Simple Syrup (see pg. 14)

METHOD
Shake all ingredients and strain into an ice-filled rocks glass. Garnish and serve.

LACANDON COCKTAIL

Colin Asare-Appiah

GLASSWARE
Large rocks

GARNISH
Fresh cilantro
Jalapeño slice

ICE
Cubes

INGREDIENTS
- 1 ounce Patron Blanco Tequila
- 1 ounce Bacardi Lime
- ¾ ounce fresh lime juice
- ¾ ounce Monin hibiscus syrup
- ¼ cup cilantro leaves
- 3 slices jalapeño
- Chilled soda to top

METHOD
Add all ingredients apart from soda into a cocktail shaker. Shake and fine-strain into an ice-filled glass. Top with soda and garnish.

PALOMA

Kimberly Hunter

GLASSWARE
Coupe

GARNISH
Edible gold flakes

ICE
Sphere

INGREDIENTS
- 2 ounces blanco Tequila
- 1 ounce fresh grapefruit juice
- ½ ounce Lime Saccharum (see right)
- 1 ounce Chambord
- Grapefruit soda, to top

METHOD

Pour the Chambord in the bottom of a coupe glass and add an ice sphere. In a shaker, add the tequila, grapefruit juice, Lime Saccharum, and ice. Shake vigorously until the shaker is chilled. Strain over an ice sphere. Sprinkle in edible gold flakes and serve.

SPECIAL INGREDIENTS

Lime Saccharum: 1 cup packed lime peels (try to avoid the white pith as much as possible) • ¾ cup sugar

Combine the lime peels and sugar in a bowl. Muddle the ingredients together for about 5 minutes to incorporate the sugar into the peels and release the natural oils from the peels. Let the muddled peels sit with the sugar for a minimum of 6 hours (but no more than 24 hours), mashing the mixture every hour for about 5 minutes each time. Strain the lime peels. Store in an airtight container in the refrigerator for up to one month.

ROSY PALOMA

Kimberly Hunter

GLASSWARE
Highball

GARNISH
Edible rose
Dehydrated grapefruit wheel

ICE
Cubes

INGREDIENTS
- 2 ounces blanco Tequila
- ½ ounce fresh lime juice
- ½ ounce rose water
- 1 ounce Chambord
- Grapefruit soda

METHOD

In a shaker, add blanco tequila, lime juice, rose water, and ice. Shake vigorously for about 10 seconds. Fill a highball glass with ice and strain the cocktail into the glass. Top with Chambord and grapefruit soda. Garnish with an edible rose and dehydrated grapefruit wheel and serve.

Rum/Ron/Rhum

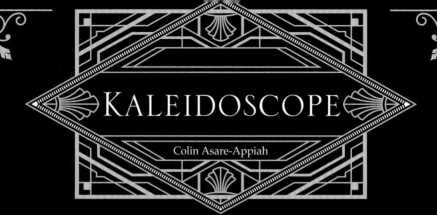

KALEIDOSCOPE

Colin Asare-Appiah

GLASSWARE
Large wine glass

GARNISH
Toasted coconut
Cherry
Pinch allspice

ICE
Crushed

INGREDIENTS
- 1 ounce Bacardi Coconut Rum
- 1 ounce Bacardi Pineapple Rum
- 1 ounce coconut water
- 2 barspoons Coco Lopez
- ½ fresh avocado
- 2 ounces fresh pineapple juice
- Toasted coconut flakes
- Dash sesame oil

METHOD
Place all ingredients in a blender and blend. Pour into Highball glass and garnish.

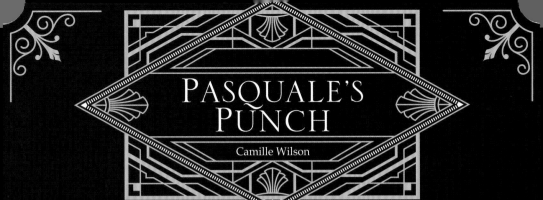

PASQUALE'S PUNCH

Camille Wilson

GLASSWARE
Coupe

GARNISH
None

ICE
Cubes

INGREDIENTS
- 1 ounce pineapple juice
- ¾ ounce Cinnamon Syrup
- ½ ounce lime juice
- ¾ ounce amaro liqueur
- 1½ ounces dark Rum

METHOD
Combine all ingredients in a cocktail shaker with ice and shake until chilled. Pour into a glass and serve.

SPECIAL INGREDIENTS

Cinnamon Sugar: 2 cups water • 4 Saigon cinnamon sticks • 1½ cups organic sugar

Add the water and cinnamon to a 1½ quart pan and bring to a boil. Reduce the heat and let the mixture simmer for about 10 minutes, then carefully strain out the cinnamon sticks. Bring the cinnamon water back to a boil. While stirring, add the sugar, and continue stirring until the sugar is dissolved. Let cool and store in an airtight container. Refrigerate until ready to use.

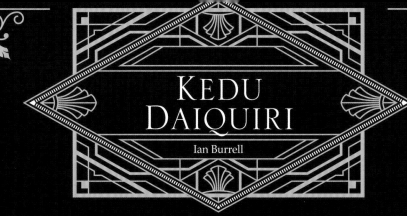

KEDU DAIQUIRI

Ian Burrell

GLASSWARE
Coupe or martini

GARNISH
Pineapple leaf

ICE
Cubes

INGREDIENTS
- 2 ounces Equiano Rum
- 1 ounce freshly squeezed lime juice
- ½ oz Piña Reàl pineapple syrup
- 3 dashes cocoa or chocolate bitters
- Champagne float

METHOD
Place all ingredients, except champagne, in a shaker tin. Add ice and shake vigorously to marry the ingredients and chill the beverage. Strain into a glass and float a little champagne on top of the cocktail. Float a pineapple leaf as a garnish and serve.

RHUBARB MOJITO

Kimberly Hunter

GLASSWARE
Highball

GARNISH
Rhubarb ribbons
Mint leaves

ICE
Crushed or fine

INGREDIENTS
- 2 ounces Bacardi Superior Rum
- 1½ ounces Rhubarb Syrup
- ¾ ounce fresh lime juice
- 3–4 mint leaves
- Club soda, to top

METHOD
In a glass, muddle the mint and lime juice. Stir in the rhubarb syrup and rum. Add ice to the glass and top with club soda. Garnish with rhubarb ribbons and mint leaves and serve.

SPECIAL INGREDIENTS

Rhubarb Syrup: **2 pounds rhubarb • 4 cups water • 1¾ cups organic sugar**

Rinse the rhubarb well and chop off the ends. Cut into small pieces and place in a medium saucepan. Add the water to the pan and bring the mixture to a boil. Reduce the heat and let simmer for 25 minutes, checking periodically to remove any particles or foam forming on the top. Remove from the heat and strain the rhubarb liquid into another saucepan. Add the sugar to the liquid, stir, and bring to a boil. When the sugar has dissolved, reduce the heat and let simmer for 5 more minutes. Remove from the heat, let cool, and then store in an airtight container. Refrigerate until ready to use.

REDENBACHER OLD-FASHIONED

Glendon Hartley

GLASSWARE
Tumbler or old-fashioned

GARNISH
Popcorn
Orange peel

ICE
Large cubes

INGREDIENTS
- 2 ounces Popcorn-Infused Rum (see below)
- 1 dash Angostura bitters
- 1 dash Regan's Orange bitters
- ½ ounce Demerara Sugar Syrup (see below)

METHOD
Place large ice cube into a tumbler or old-fashioned glass. Add all liquid ingredients to a mixing glass, add ice, and stir until diluted and chilled. Strain all liquid ingredients into a tumbler glass with ice. Garnish with the fresh popcorn and orange zest and serve.

SPECIAL INGREDIENTS

Popcorn-Infused Rum:

Pop one bag of microwave butter popcorn and place contents into a large ziplock bag. Pour one 750 mL bottle of Bacardi 8 Year Reserva Ocho Rum to infuse overnight. After one night, place the bag in the freezer until all fats and solids are frozen (approximately 4–6 hours). After all fats and solids are frozen, cut a small hole in the bottom of the bag and strain through the coffee filter. Using multiple coffee filters will yield the best results.

Demerara Sugar Syrup: 400 g (1½ cups plus 2 tablespoons) water • 800 g (4 cups) Demerara sugar

Note: For this recipe, measuring the ingredients by weight rather than by volume is more accurate.

Heat the water over medium-high heat until a light steam is visible, then stir in the sugar until dissolved. Let cool and store in an airtight container. Refrigerate until ready to use.

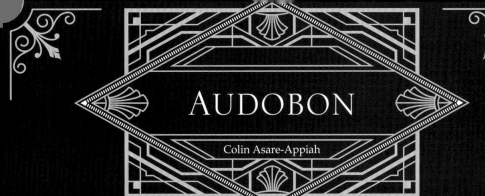

AUDOBON

Colin Asare-Appiah

GLASSWARE
Martini

GARNISH
Orange twist
Raspberries
Mint sprig

ICE
Cubes

INGREDIENTS
• 2 ounces Banks 5 Rum
• 2 ounces rooibos tea
• ½ ounce Monin raspberry syrup
• 3 slices fresh ginger
• 1 egg white

METHOD
Place all ingredients in a blender and blend. Pour into Highball glass and garnish.

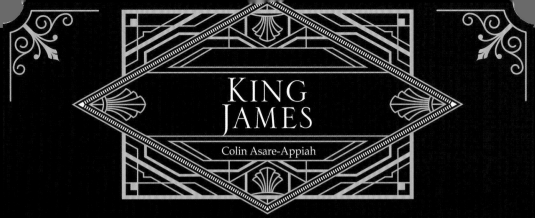

KING JAMES

Colin Asare-Appiah

GLASSWARE
Highball

GARNISH
Lemon wheel
Cherry

ICE
Cubes

INGREDIENTS
- 1 ounce Santa Teresa Rum
- 1 ounce Banks 7 Rum
- ½ ounce Martini Fiero
- 1 ounce mango juice
- 1 ounce lychee juice
- ½ ounce Ginger Syrup (see below)
- ½ ounce fresh lime juice
- 3 dashes orange bitters
- 2 barspoons hazelnut and chocolate spread

METHOD
Add all ingredients into a cocktail shaker. Shake and strain over ice. Garnish and serve.

SPECIAL INGREDIENTS

Ginger Syrup: 1⅓ cup chopped ginger • 2 ¾ cup water • ¾ cup organic sugar

Combine the ginger, water, and sugar in a 1½ quart saucepan and bring to a boil. Stir the mixture until the sugar is dissolved. Let stand, covered, for half an hour. Strain into an airtight container to remove all particles. Refrigerate until ready to use.

BLACK STAR

Colin Asare-Appiah

GLASSWARE
Martini

GARNISH
3 coffee beans

ICE
Cubes

INGREDIENTS
- 2 ounces Banks 7 Rum
- 1 ounce Bouvery chocolate liqueur
- ½ ounce Monin raspberry syrup
- 2 ounces espresso
- Pinch salt

METHOD
Pour all ingredients into a cocktail tin and add ice. Shake and strain. Garnish with 3 coffee beans and serve.

QUIET STORM
AKA LULUCOLINS

Colin Asare-Appiah

GLASSWARE
Highball

GARNISH
Lime wedge

ICE
Cubes

INGREDIENTS
- 2 ounces Bacardi 8 Year Reserva Ocho Rum
- 1 ounce Domaine de Canton ginger liqueur
- ½ ounce Simple Syrup (see pg. 14)
- ½ lime cut into 4 pieces
- 4 dashes Angostura bitters
- Ginger beer

METHOD
Muddle limes in a cocktail shaker. Add all ingredients and shake. Pour into highball glass. Fill with ice and top with ginger beer. Garnish and serve.

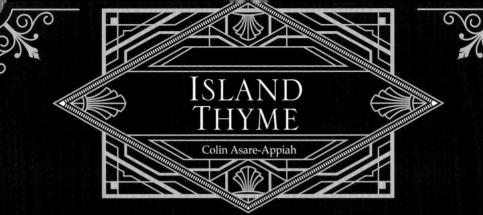

ISLAND THYME

Colin Asare-Appiah

GLASSWARE
Highball

GARNISH
Red pepper slices
Carrot slices
Thyme sprig

ICE
Cubes

INGREDIENTS
- ½ ounce Bacardi Superior Rum
- ½ ounce Wray & Nephew Rum
- ½ ounce fresh lime
- 2 ounces carrot juice
- 2 ounces red bell pepper (blend pieces)
- ½ ounce Simple Syrup (see pg. 14)

METHOD
Pour all the ingredients into a cocktail shaker. Shake and strain into an ice-filled glass. Cap with crushed ice, garnish, and serve.

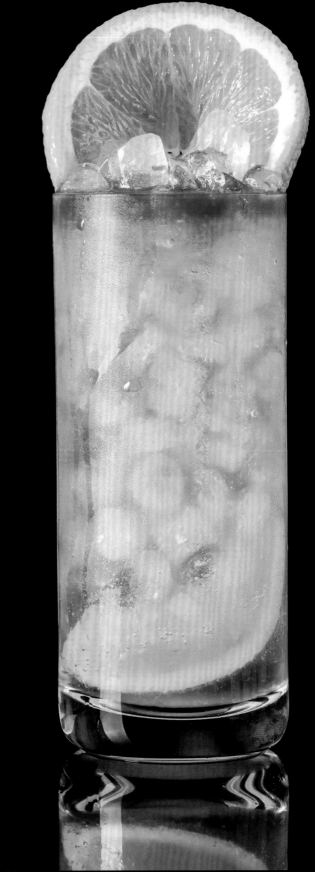

JOY'S COCKTAIL

Joy Spence

GLASSWARE
Highball

GARNISH
Orange peel

ICE
Cubes

INGREDIENTS
- Orange slice
- 1 ounce Appleton Estate 8 Year Reserve Rum
- 3 ounces ginger ale
- Slice of orange
- 5 drops Angostura bitters

METHOD
Squeeze the orange slice into a highball glass, drop it into the glass, and muddle it. Add ice, build the remaining ingredients, and stir. Garnish with an orange peel and serve.

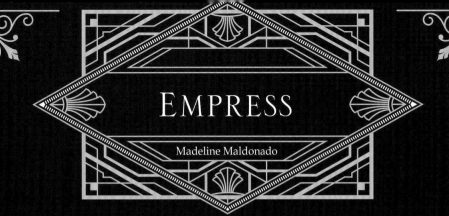

EMPRESS

Madeline Maldonado

GLASSWARE
Coupe

GARNISH
None

ICE
Cubes

INGREDIENTS
- 2 ounces Boukman Botanical Rhum
- ¾ ounce lime juice
- ¾ ounce Simple Syrup (see pg. 14)
- Pinch of salt
- Fee Brothers foam
- Lambrusco to float

METHOD
Add all ingredients except the Lambrusco into a shaker. Dry-shake first, then add ice and shake again. Pour into a coupe or martini glass. Add Lambrusco on top.

MAI TAI

Joy Spence

GLASSWARE
Tropical

GARNISH
Edible flower

ICE
Cubes

INGREDIENTS
- 2 ounces Appleton Estate 8 Year Reserve Rum
- ½ ounce fresh lime juice
- ½ ounce orange Curaçao
- ½ ounce orgeat (almond) syrup

METHOD
Shake all ingredients and strain over ice in a tropical glass. Garnish and serve.

HOT BUTTERED RUM

Marlena "Miko" Richardson

GLASSWARE
Toddy

GARNISH
Grated cinnamon

ICE
Cubes

INGREDIENTS
- 3 ounces spiced Rum
- 1½ ounces butterscotch schnapps
- 1½ ounces vanilla creamer or milk; if milk is used, add splash of vanilla extract

METHOD
Shake over ice or heat by warming creamer or milk (either way is great). Add a dash of cinnamon on top and serve.

ISLAND OUTPOST

Colin Asare-Appiah

GLASSWARE
Toddy

GARNISH
Lime slice
Cinnamon stick

ICE
None

INGREDIENTS
- 1 ounce Bacardi Gold Rum
- 1 tea bag of moringa leaves
- 2 slices fresh ginger
- ¾ ounce Simple Syrup (see pg. 14)
- Pinch allspice
- ¾ cup warm water

METHOD
Pour all ingredients into a toddy glass. Stir with cinnamon sticks and serve.

JAMAICAN DAIQUIRI

Joy Spence

GLASSWARE
Coupe

GARNISH
None

ICE
Cubes

INGREDIENTS
- 2 ounces Appleton Signature Blend Rum
- ¾ ounce fresh lime juice
- ½ ounce Simple Syrup (see pg. 14) or demerara

METHOD
Place all ingredients into an ice-filled cocktail shaker. Shake vigorously, strain into a chilled coupe glass, and serve.

COGNAC

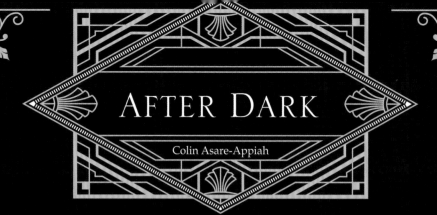

After Dark

Colin Asare-Appiah

Glassware
Chilled martini

Garnish
Orange twist
Powdered chocolate

Ice
Crushed

Ingredients
- 1 ounce D'USSÉ VSOP Cognac
- 1 ounce Crème de Cacao
- 1 ounce Crème de Menthe
- 2 ounces heavy cream
- 2 dashes Hella bitters chocolate

Method
Pour all ingredients into a blender with 1 cup crushed ice. Blend slowly. Fine-strain into a chilled martini glass. Sprinkle powdered chocolate on top, garnish with an orange twist, and serve.

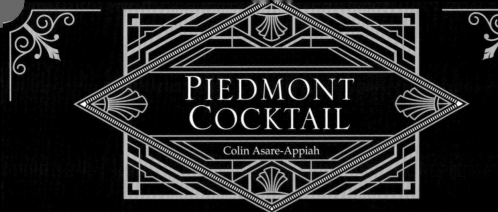

PIEDMONT COCKTAIL

Colin Asare-Appiah

GLASSWARE
Julep

GARNISH
Rosemary sprig
Cocktail cherry dusted with powdered sugar

ICE
Crushed

INGREDIENTS
• 1 ounce D'USSÉ Cognac
• 1 barspoon yellow Chartreuse
• ½ ounce fresh lemon juice
• 1 barspoon vanilla syrup
• 2 dashes Hella bitters eucalyptus
• Top with Martini Asti

METHOD
Place ingredients in an ice-filled shaker. Use cube ice to shake and then strain over crushed ice. Top with Martini Asti. Garnish and serve.

HENNESSY SIDECAR

Alexis Brown

GLASSWARE
Martini

GARNISH
Expressed orange peel
Sugar rim

ICE
Cubes

INGREDIENTS
- 1½ ounces Hennessy VSOP Cognac
- ¾ ounce Grand Marnier
- ½ ounce lemon juice

METHOD
Sugar the rim of a martini glass. Add all ingredients to a shaker tin. Add ice and shake vigorously, then strain into the sugar-rimmed glass. Express an orange peel and serve.

COOL RUNNINGS

Colin Asare-Appiah

GLASSWARE
Highball

GARNISH
Dusted with allspice

ICE
Cubes

INGREDIENTS
- 2 ounces D'USSÉ Cognac
- ½ ounce Myris Nutmeg Liqueur
- 2 ounces Condensed Milk
- 1 ounce Milk
- ¼ ounce Vanilla extract
- 3 ounces Guinness Extra Stout

METHOD
Blend all ingredients with ice and pour into a Highball glass. Garnish with a dust of allspice.

GIN

BUZZWORD

Vance Henderson

GLASSWARE
Rocks

GARNISH
2 cucumber rounds

ICE
Cubes

INGREDIENTS
- 1 ounce Hendrick's Gin
- ¾ ounce fresh lemon juice
- ¾ ounce Drambuie
- ¾ ounce Dolin Blanc vermouth

METHOD
Combine all ingredients in a cocktail shaker with ice. Shake very well and strain over fresh ice into a rocks glass. Garnish with two cucumber rounds and serve.

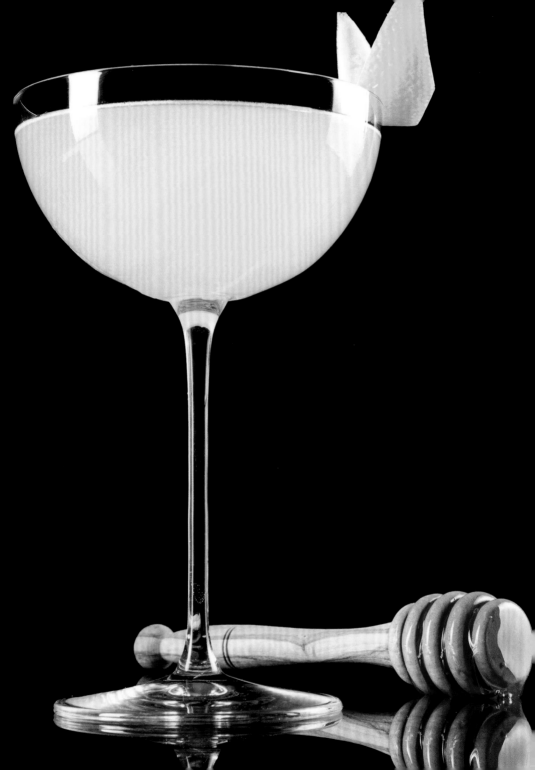

BEE'S KNEES

Vance Henderson

GLASSWARE
Chilled coupe

GARNISH
Lemon twist

ICE
Cubes

INGREDIENTS
- 2 ounces Gin
- ¾ ounce lemon juice
- ½ ounce Organic Honey Syrup (see below)

METHOD
Combine all ingredients in a cocktail shaker with ice. Shake very well and strain into a chilled coupe glass. Garnish with a lemon twist and serve.

SPECIAL INGREDIENTS

Organic Honey Syrup: 1 cup organic honey • 1 cup water

Combine the honey and water in a saucepan over medium-high heat. Bring to a boil and boil until the honey is dissolved. Remove the mixture from the heat and let cool. Store the cooled syrup in an airtight container in the refrigerator.

LAST WORD

Vance Henderson

GLASSWARE
Chilled coupe

GARNISH
Maraschino cherry

ICE
TK

INGREDIENTS
- 1 ounce Gin
- 1 ounce green Chartreuse
- 1 ounce lime juice
- 1 ounce maraschino cherry liqueur

METHOD
Combine all ingredients in a cocktail shaker with ice. Shake very well and strain into a chilled coupe glass. Garnish with a maraschino cherry and serve.

GIN DANDY

Colin Asare-Appiah

GLASSWARE
Chilled martini

GARNISH
Basil leaf

ICE
Cubes

INGREDIENTS
- 1½ ounce Oxley Gin
- 1 ounce Martini Bianco
- 1 ounce apple cider
- ½ ounce fresh lemon juice
- ½ ounce Monin granny smith apple syrup
- 3 basil leaves

METHOD
Add all the ingredients into an ice-filled shaker. Shake and strain into a chilled martini glass. Garnish with a basil leaf and serve.

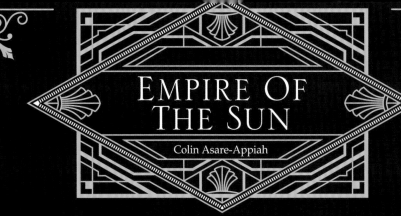

EMPIRE OF THE SUN

Colin Asare-Appiah

GLASSWARE
Highball

GARNISH
Basil leaf
Thai chili

ICE
Crushed

INGREDIENTS
- 1 ½ ounces Bombay Sapphire Gin
- ½ ounce Suze liqueur
- ¾ ounce fresh lime juice
- ½ ounce Monin turmeric syrup
- 1 Thai chili, chopped with seeds
- 2 basil leaves
- Prosecco

METHOD
Place all ingredients into a cocktail tin. Add ice and shake. Fine-strain through a sieve into an ice-filled highball glass. Top off with prosecco. Garnish with basil leaf and Thai chili (these can be taken from the sieve), and serve.

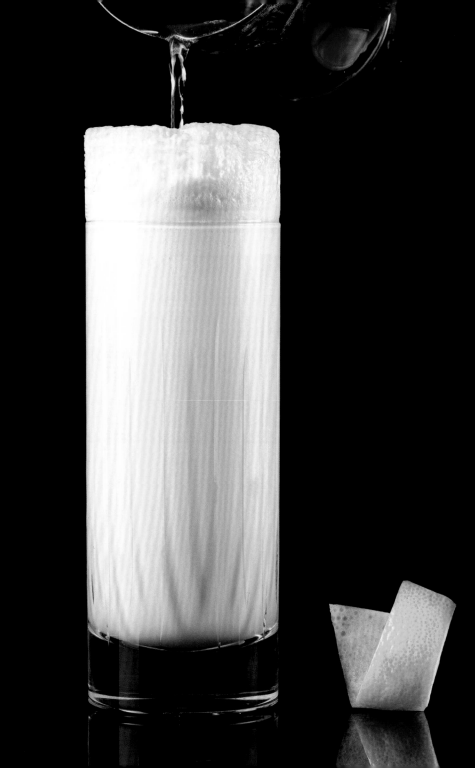

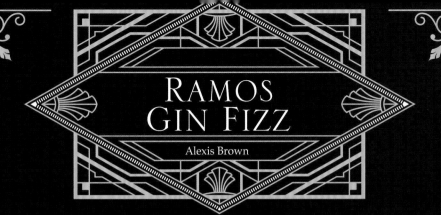

Ramos Gin Fizz

Alexis Brown

Glassware
Highball

Garnish
Expressed lemon oil

Ice
Large cubes

Ingredients
- 1½ ounces London dry Gin
- ½ ounce lemon juice
- ½ ounce lime juice
- 1 ounce Simple Syrup (see pg. 14)
- 1 ounce heavy cream
- 2 drops rose water
- 1 egg white
- Soda water

Method
Starting with the egg whites, build all ingredients except the soda. Dry-shake (no ice) for a minimum of 2 minutes to achieve maximum froth. Add 3 large ice cubes (1×1 inch) and shake until the ice fully dissolves. Pour the contents into a highball glass to about 1 inch under the rim. Keep the remaining cocktail in the shaker. Tap the glass on the bar top and allow to sit for 1 minute to settle. Patience is key here! Splash soda into the tin with the remaining cocktail and swish around. After 1 minute, pour the remaining contents in the tin directly in the center of the cocktail and watch as the foam head rises. Garnish with expressed lemon oil and serve with a straw.

ELDERFLOWER GIN FIZZ

Jaylynn Little

GLASSWARE
Champagne flute

GARNISH
Lemon twist

ICE
Cubes

INGREDIENTS
- 1½ ounces Tanqueray Gin
- 1 ounce Saint Germain elderflower liqueur
- 1 ounce fresh lemon juice
- 1 cup ice
- Prosecco, chilled

METHOD
Add the gin, Saint Germain, lemon juice, and 1 cup of ice to a shaker or jar with a lid and shake until chilled. Strain and pour the cocktail into a champagne flute, top off with chilled prosecco, and serve.

LABADI

Colin Asare-Appiah

GLASSWARE
Champagne

GARNISH
Lemon twist

ICE
Cubes

INGREDIENTS
- 1 ounce Bombay Sapphire Gin
- 1 dash pastis
- Juice of ½ lemon
- Barspoon of lavender sugar
- Champagne

METHOD
Add gin, lemon, pastis (optional), and Lavender Sugar into an ice-filled shaker. Shake vigorously. Fine-strain into a champagne glass, top off with champagne, and serve.

SUNRISE WITH POST

Birdie Brown Plain Hooch

GLASSWARE

Rocks

GARNISH

Grapefruit wedge

ICE

Large cubes

INGREDIENTS

- 2 ounces Birdie Brown Plain Hooch
- 1 ounce fresh grapefruit juice
- 1 lime wedge
- Pinch kosher salt

METHOD

Fill a rocks glass with ice and pour in grapefruit juice. Add Birdie Brown Plain Hooch. Squeeze a lime wedge and drop inside and add a pinch of kosher salt on top. Garnish with a grapefruit wedge and serve.

VODKA

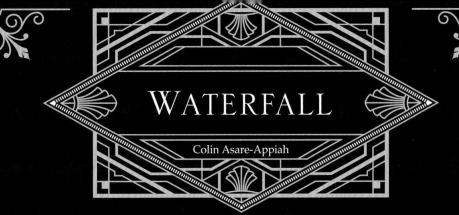

WATERFALL

Colin Asare-Appiah

GLASSWARE
Highball

GARNISH
Mint leaves
Lemon twist

ICE
Cubes

INGREDIENTS
- 2 ounces Grey Goose Vodka
- 1 ounce Martini Bianco
- 6 mint leaves
- ½ ounce fresh lemon juice
- ½ ounce Monin habanero syrup
- 1 ounce pineapple puree
- Soda water to top

METHOD
Muddle the mint in a cocktail shaker and then pour in the rest of the ingredients. Shake and strain into an ice-filled highball glass. Garnish with mint and a lemon twist and serve.

ROSE GARDEN

Colin Asare-Appiah

GLASSWARE
Champagne

GARNISH
Rose petal

ICE
Cubes

INGREDIENTS
- 1 ounce Grey Goose Vodka
- ½ ounce ruby red grapefruit juice
- 1 barspoons granulated sugar
- 2 barspoons rose petal preserves/confit

METHOD
Add vodka, sugar, grapefruit, and preserves and shake over ice. Fine-strain into a champagne glass. Top with champagne, garnish, and serve.

FRUIT LOOPS

Colin Asare-Appiah

GLASSWARE
Highball

GARNISH
Citrus twist
Maraschino cherry

ICE
Cubes

INGREDIENTS
- 3 ounces pineapple juice
- 2 ounces orange juice
- 1 ounce cranberry juice
- ½ ounce Grenadine Syrup (see right)
- 2 ounces Absolut Citron Vodka

METHOD
Combine vodka and juices in a chilled highball glass with ice and stir well. Add Grenadine Syrup and garnish with citrus twist and maraschino cherry.

SPECIAL INGREDIENTS

Grenadine Syrup: 1 cup organic sugar
2 cups pomegranate juice (preferably fresh)
2 tablespoons fresh-squeezed lemon juice

Combine the sugar and juices in a 1½ quart saucepan and bring to a boil. Reduce the heat and stir until the mixture thickens. (For a thinner consistency, add a little water.) Let cool, then store in an airtight container. Refrigerate until ready to use.

TURMERIC TONIC

Colin Asare-Appiah

GLASSWARE
Collins

GARNISH
Lemon wedge
Cayenne pepper

ICE
Cubes

INGREDIENTS
- 1 2-inch piece peeled turmeric
- 1 2-inch piece peeled ginger
- ½ lemon
- 3 tablespoons agave nectar
- 12 ounces lemon seltzer water
- 2 ounces Vodka

METHOD
Pass turmeric, ginger, and lemon (with the peel) through a juicer and collect the fresh juice in a container. Evenly pour 2 tablespoons of the mixture over ice into two Collins glasses, add 2 ounces of vodka to each, and lightly stir. Top each glass with lemon seltzer water and add a dash of cayenne pepper and lemon wedge to garnish.

VICTORY LAP

Joseph Samuel

GLASSWARE
Coupe

GARNISH
Expressed and discarded lemon twist

ICE
Cubes

INGREDIENTS
- 1½ ounces Grey Goose Vodka
- 1 ounce blue Curaçao
- ¾ ounce Lemongrass Syrup (see right)
- ¾ ounce lemon
- 1 egg white

METHOD
Place all ingredients into a shaker without ice. Dry shake (without ice), and add ice. Shake vigorously again. Strain into a chilled coupe, garnish with an expressed and discarded lemon twist and serve.

SPECIAL INGREDIENTS

Lemongrass Syrup: ½ pint water
4 stalks diced lemongrass • 1 cup of superfine sugar

Heat the water, add sugar, and stir until its dissolved. Add lemongrass and leave on a slow simmer for 10 minutes.

SUI GENERIS

Colin Asare-Appiah

GLASSWARE
Highball

GARNISH
Blood orange slice
Frozen cranberries

ICE
Cubes

INGREDIENTS
- 2 tablespoons Blood Orange Syrup (see right)
- 1 cup ginger beer
- ½ cup cranberry juice
- 2 ounces vodka

METHOD
Combine cranberry juice, Blood Orange Syrup, and vodka in a highball glass. Stir well and top with ginger beer. Garnish with frozen cranberries and blood orange slice and serve.

SPECIAL INGREDIENTS

Blood Orange Syrup: ½ cup fresh-squeezed blood orange juice • ⅓ cup organic sugar • 4 sprigs fresh thyme

Add blood orange juice, sugar, and thyme in a medium saucepan and bring to a simmer over medium heat. Stir occasionally to dissolve the sugar. Let cook for 2 minutes to infuse flavors. Remove from heat and let cool to room temperature. Once cool, strain the syrup through a sieve into an airtight container. Refrigerate until ready to use.

PUNCHES

TINGS ARE JUST PEACHY

Karl Franz

GLASSWARE
Punch bowl

GARNISH
Lemon slices

ICE
Cubes

INGREDIENTS
- 1 part freshly squeezed lemon juice
- 1 part Cinnamon Syrup (see below)
- 1 part Ginger Syrup (see below)
- 1 part Combier peach liqueur
- 3 parts Teeling Small Batch Irish Whisky
- 3 parts unsweetened freshly brewed green tea
- 12 dashes Angostura bitters

METHOD
Combine all ingredients in a punch bowl. Stir with large ice cubes and add garnish. Serve chilled.

SPECIAL INGREDIENTS

Cinnamon Syrup: 2 cups water • 4 Saigon cinnamon sticks • 1½ cups organic sugar

Add the water and cinnamon to a 1½ quart pan and bring to a boil. Reduce the heat and let the mixture simmer for about 10 minutes, then carefully strain out the cinnamon sticks. Bring the cinnamon water back to a boil. While stirring, add the sugar, and continue stirring until the sugar is dissolved. Let cool and store in an airtight container. Refrigerate until ready to use.

Ginger Syrup: ⅓ cup chopped ginger • ¾ cup water • ¾ cup organic sugar

Combine the ginger, water, and sugar in a 1½ quart saucepan and bring to a boil. Stir the mixture until the sugar is dissolved. Let stand, covered, for half an hour. Strain into an airtight container to remove all particles. Refrigerate until ready to use.

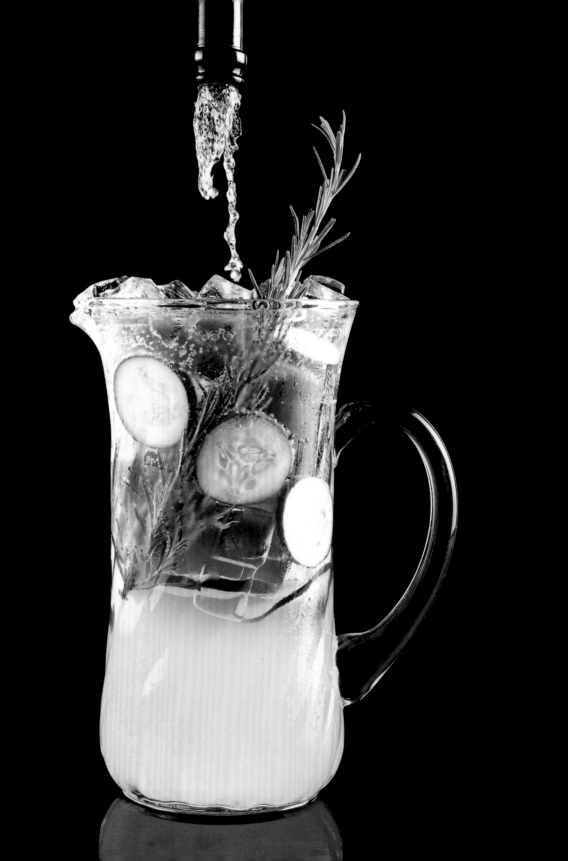

VANILLA SKY

Colin Asare-Appiah

GLASSWARE
Pitcher (serves 4)

GARNISH
Rosemary
Cucumber slices

ICE
Cubes

INGREDIENTS
• 4 ounces Martini Bianco
• 4 ounces Saint Germain elderflower liqueur
• 4 ounces Noilly Prat vermouth
• 6 ounces lemonade
• 1 ounce Monin vanilla syrup
• Top with prosecco

METHOD
Add all ingredients into a pitcher. Stir and fill with ice, then top with prosecco. Garnish and serve.

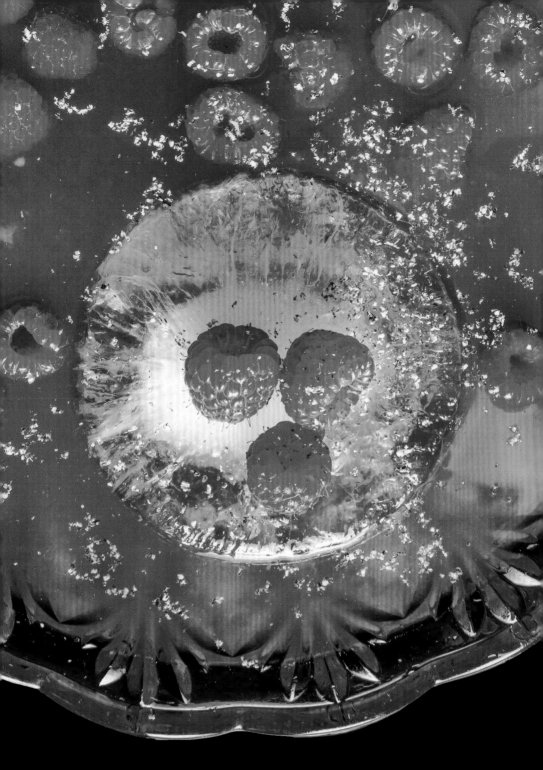

PORCHLIGHT

Colin Asare-Appiah

GLASSWARE
Punch bowl (serves 6)

GARNISH
Grated nutmeg
1 cup raspberries

ICE
Large ice block (freeze water in Tupperware)

INGREDIENTS
- 6 ounces Stillhouse black Bourbon
- 6 ounces Stillhouse moonshine
- 2 ounces peach liqueur
- 2 ounces Crème Yvette
- 18 ounces Earl Grey tea, steeped
- 6 ounces raspberry purée
- 6 ounces fresh lemon juice
- 6 ounces Monin cinnamon syrup
- 4 ounces soda water
- 8 dashes orange bitters

METHOD
Pour all ingredients into a large punch bowl. Stir vigorously, add ice, and add garnishes. Stir and serve.

OTHER BEVERAGES

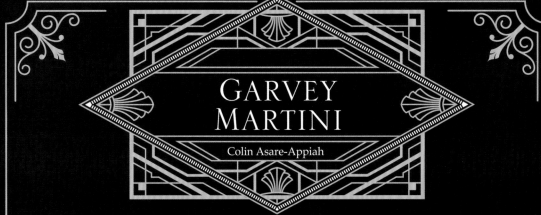

GARVEY MARTINI

Colin Asare-Appiah

Martini

GARNISH
Star anise

ICE
Cubes

INGREDIENTS
- 2 ounces Grey Goose Essences
- ½ ounce green Chartreuse
- ½ ounce fresh lime
- 2 ounces Homemade Sorrell (see below)

METHOD
Shake all ingredients and then fine-strain into a chilled martini glass. Garnish and serve.

SPECIAL INGREDIENTS

Homemade Sorrel: 6 cups water • 5 cloves • 5 balls allspice • 2 star anise or ½ teaspoon anise seeds

1 knuckle ginger, sliced • 1 cup hibiscus tea leaves • ½ cup raw sugar (any sugar can substitute)

Bring the water to a boil over high heat and add cloves, allspice, anise, and ginger. Reduce heat to medium and allow to slow boil for 3–4 minutes. Reduce heat again and add hibiscus leaves and sugar. Stir for 2 minutes, turn off heat, and let cool to room temperature. When chilled, add to ice and serve. Feel free to add your favorite rum.

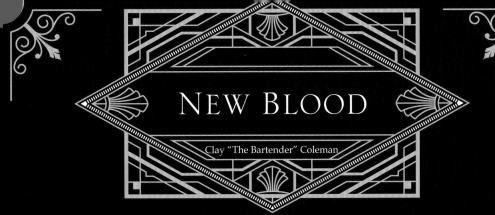

NEW BLOOD

Clay "The Bartender" Coleman

GLASSWARE
Double rocks

GARNISH
Sea salt rim
Blood orange wheel

ICE
Cubes

INGREDIENTS
- 6 dashes chocolate bitters
- ¾ ounce Bouvery chocolate liqueur
- ¾ ounce Cointreau
- ½ ounce lime juice
- ¾ ounce blood orange juice
- 1½ ounce Mezcal
- 2 deseeded jalapeño slices, muddled
- Chocolate bar

METHOD
Shake all ingredients except the chocolate bar with ice in a shaker and fine-strain over ice into a double rocks glass with a sea salt rim. Using a fruit zester, grate the side of the chocolate bar over the cocktail to garnish with chocolate dust. Complete the garnish with a blood orange wheel and serve.

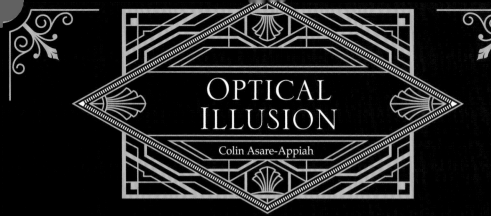

OPTICAL ILLUSION

Colin Asare-Appiah

GLASSWARE
Large rocks

GARNISH
Mint sprig

ICE
Crushed

INGREDIENTS
• 1 ounce Leblon Cachaça
• 1 ounce Saint Germain elderflower liqueur
• 1 barspoon granulated sugar
• 1 lemon, cut into 8 pieces

METHOD
Strain all ingredients in an ice-filled large rocks glass. Garnish and serve.

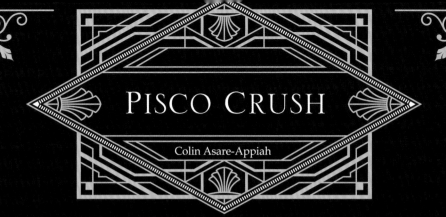

PISCO CRUSH

Colin Asare-Appiah

GLASSWARE
Large rocks

GARNISH
Lemon slice

ICE
Crushed

INGREDIENTS
- 2 ounces Barsol Pisco
- 4 white grapes, cut in half
- ½ ounce Simple Syrup (see pg. 14)
- ½ ounce fresh lemon juice

METHOD
Gently muddle the grapes in a cocktail tin. Place all other ingredients in a shaker and dry-shake (without ice). Pour into a rocks glass, add crushed ice, and use the back of a barspoon to stir. Garnish with a lemon slice and serve.

POINSETTIA

Marlena "Miko" Richardson

GLASSWARE
Champagne flute

GARNISH
Orange slice

ICE
None

INGREDIENTS
- ½ ounce Cointreau or triple sec
- 3 ounces cranberry juice
- Champagne to top

METHOD
Pour Cointreau and cranberry juice into a chilled champagne flute. Stir thoroughly, top with champagne and an orange twist, and serve.

MASON'S STABLE

Colin Asare-Appiah

GLASSWARE
Rocks

GARNISH
Orange twist
Cocktail cherry

ICE
Cubes

INGREDIENTS
- 2 ounces Calvados
- 1 ounce Bénédictine herbal liqueur
- 1 ounce tamarind juice
- 2 dashes Bittercube Bolivar Bitters

METHOD
Stir all ingredients over ice in a cocktail shaker. Strain into an ice-filled rocks glass, garnish, and serve.

RUNAWAY BEACH

Colin Asare-Appiah

GLASSWARE
Tropical

GARNISH
Lime wheel
Sugar-dusted mint leaf

ICE
Crushed

INGREDIENTS
• 1 ounce Bacardi Banana Rum
• 1 ounce Leblon Cachaça
• ½ ounce Bénédictine herbal liqueur
• ¾ ounce fresh lime
• 1 ounce pineapple juice
• ½ ounce Cinnamon Syrup (see right)
• 2 dashes Angostura Rum

METHOD
Add all ingredients to a cocktail shaker over cubed ice. Shake and strain. Fill with crushed ice, garnish, and serve.

SPECIAL INGREDIENTS

Cinnamon Syrup: 2 cups water • 4 Saigon cinnamon sticks • 1½ cups organic sugar

Add the water and cinnamon to a 1½ quart pan and bring to a boil. Reduce the heat and let the mixture simmer for about 10 minutes, then carefully strain out the cinnamon sticks. Bring the cinnamon water back to a boil. While stirring, add the sugar, and continue stirring until the sugar is dissolved. Let cool and store in an airtight container. Refrigerate until ready to use.

SHAMAR

Colin Asare-Appiah

GLASSWARE
Highball

GARNISH
Orange slice

ICE
Cubes

INGREDIENTS
• 2 ounces Martini bitter
• 1 ounce Blended Family Raspberry liqueur
• ½ ounce fresh lime juice
• Top with Pink Ting soda

METHOD
Shake all ingredients: Pour into ice filled Highball glass. Cap with ice and top with Pink Ting soda.

Voices Of Black Mixcellence

"I really love the versatility of gin. That's what makes it one of my favorites."
—Alexis Brown - Chicago, IL

"You can sit and sip whiskey...it's the mature thing to do. I guess it's like my personality."
—"Bartender Barry" Johnson - Philadelphia, PA

"Rum is medicine. Rum is something you cook with. Rum has been a part of my life for so long, and I love the smell of it."
—Camille Wilson - Brooklyn, NY

"Being a barback first ultimately makes you a better bartender."
—Clay "the Bartender" Coleman - Oakland, California

"The industry is changing, and we need to make sure we are constantly part of the narrative at all times."
—Colin Asare-Appiah - New York, NY

"Rum can be light. It can be dark. It can be nonchalant and subtle or add a big punch to your drink."
—Nigal Vann - Chicago, IL

"There are people who talk to me like I have some kind of magical power because I'm the bartender. Anything that requires any skill that you develop, you get better the more you do it."
—Ed "the Ed Experience" Warner II - Houston, TX

"I take my job very seriously. I let my work speak for me. If you enjoy what you're doing, people will love what you do."
—Miguel Soto Rincon - Tampa, FL

"If we bring in lemons, we'll be using the lemon skins, the lemon peels, the lemon pulp for sorbet or something, and then the juice. Maybe it's for ceviche. Maybe it's clarified juice. We are going to use it all."
—Glendon Hartley - Washington, D.C.

"That's what we do in the Caribbean. We tell stories."
—Ian Burrell - London, England

"People are going to come out of this [pandemic] being the bomb home bartenders."
—Jaylynn Little - Silver Spring, MD

"I see a lot of bartenders doing new things every day. Some of the things I see, I add into my repertoire to keep my skills sharp."
—Joe Samuel - Dallas, TX

"In a hot climate such as Jamaica's, you're getting all the flavors being developed at a faster rate. The vanilla, coffee, cocoa, spicy, nutty flavors are created faster, the taste is smoother, and the aftertaste is sweeter."
—Joy Spence - Nassau Valley, Jamaica

"Mixology is a performance art in how you prepare the cocktail. It's a culinary art in terms of the way it's presented. It's alchemy in putting together the flavors and all the profiles."
—Karl Franz Williams - New York, NY

"When people meet me, they often make comments like, 'Oh, we had no idea a Black woman was doing this' or 'that a Black woman owned this business' and are often pleasantly surprised by my work."
—Kimberly Hunter - Dallas, TX

"I am the boss [of Shots by Miko]. People have to readjust themselves accordingly to speak to me sometimes after learning that. I am me and she is me."
—Marlena "Miko" Richardson - Kansas City, MO

"I call myself a modern bartender because bartending has changed so much. It's not just about making drinks or standing behind that bar anymore."
—Ms Franky Marshall - New York, NY

"Being a Black woman, I've been passed up on a lot of different jobs and positions. A lot of times I've had to work my way from the ground up."
—Dessalyn "Dea" Pierre - Brooklyn, NY

"Being Black in this industry changes every year. It went from being a token and being okay with that, to being like, 'I'm the one in the room, and I'm at the table.'"
—Tiffanie "Drinking Coach" Barriere - Atlanta, GA

"I don't just wanna make a dope cocktail—that's just the first layer. For me, I need to do research and expand on what the story is that needs to be told, because the story then influences the ingredients, the drink choice, and even the garnish, and, at the end of the day, just the experience on a whole."
—Vance Henderson - Washington, D.C.

"A Cabernet, if you look in a textbook, it's grapes, tannins, bell pepper, earth, full-bodied...but then you have to consider, Is it from a cooler climate? What's the sun exposure? What's the altitude? Who's making it? Was it aged in steel? Was it aged in oak?"
—Madeline "Maddy" Maldonado

ACKNOWLEDGEMENTS
TAMIKA HALL

I want to thank God for giving me the means to make this book happen. Without him, none of this would have been possible. None of it.

I am so thankful that I get to document the stories of my ancestors who gave their blood, sweat, and tears to build this thing we call America. Mixology is but a tiny facet of our contribution to this country, and I am honored that I can proudly say that I've created a place to share their stories. The new generation of bartenders are a force to be reckoned with and come with the same fire and drive as their ancestors did. I'm proud to give their stories a home for people to reference and draw inspiration from.

To my mom, who is my right hand in anything I do. She tirelessly supports all my crazy ideas and endeavors without question. Without her, none of this would have been possible. I am forever grateful for her and have no idea what I would do without her.

To my dad, who was the catalyst for all of this. He taught me the importance of a well-made old-fashioned, top-shelf spirits, and cocktails after a long day. He taught me the importance of quality over quantity and exhibited a model work ethic that I still draw from to this day. He told me that I was worthy of only the best that money can buy and that I should be able to buy it. The void that I feel because he isn't here is immense. Not a day goes by when I don't miss him. I know he is watching me and pulling strings from up top. My guardian angel, I love you.

To my children, who motivate me to continue to do things that they can be proud of—Sachielle, Camden, Tyler, Kiara, Taylor, and Kennedy—thank you for having the patience to allow me to put the work in. The fact that you can proudly point to something and say "My mom did that" will forever motivate me to do more.

Thank you, Marvis Johnson and Kingston Imperial / Penguin Random House, for taking a chance on me and allowing me to execute an idea that didn't seem possible.

To all the bartenders who are featured in this book—Alexis Brown, Barry Johnson, Camille Wilson, Clay Coleman, Colin Asare-Appiah, Dessalyn Pierre, Ed Warner II, Ms Franky Marshall, Glendon Hartley, Ian Burrell, Jaylynn Little, Joe Samuel, Joy Spence, Karl Franz Williams, Kimberly Hunter, Madeline Maldonado, Marlena Richardson, Miguel Soto Rincon, Nigal Vann, Tiffanie Barriere, and Vance Henderson—thank you for taking the time to interview with me, tell me your story, and trust that I would accurately represent you.

Rashaad, the little brother my parents didn't birth, love you till forever. You always have my back through whatever, and I will always have yours. Please hug Mama Linda for me.

Dee . . . Danielle Thornton, the best friend that everyone deserves. Thank you for keeping me grounded and sane through all the madness. Supporting me through the good times and dragging me when necessary. Mr. Swift . . . sir.

My higher ground, my rocket love. Eff gravity, I'd rather stay up here, but . . .

Maggie Reyes, a.k.a. Mags, you are one of a kind. We've been synced since that day on the playground in the LES. I love you forever and a day, and I thank you for all your guidance and support.

Get you some friends who will mention your name in a room and are not afraid to see you succeed. Thank you, Kathy Iandoli, for pulling up a seat for me at the literary table. But even further, you are the epitome of a fitted sheet. You held me down at a time when we both were navigating the unknown. We don't fold easily. Never have. Never will. Love and appreciate you.

Lauren LoCasio, we've been riding since kindergarten days at TNS. My ride or die, whether it's Saturday dance classes or chaperoning class trips. What would I do without you and your real-world perspective?

Sue Biello, you are an amazing person, and I am happy to call you a friend.

Danette Smith, thank you for being the big sister I never had. We were Sound Factory originals. Orange and Black party crew. Moving mattresses at all hours of the night and other embargoed shenanigans would never have happened without you.

Daisy Ramcharitar, thank you for being the literary intern I didn't know I needed.

Auntie Icey, Auntie Pat, Uncle Tony, Uncle Sid, Auntie Elaine, Auntie Vanessa, Auntie Paula, Auntie TJ, Auntie Janie . . . family is everything, and I am glad I have you guys. You've always inspired me to be the best I can be, at all times.
Auntie Yvonne, we are forever connected. Thank you for being with me for those final moments.

William Asare Appiah, Dimitri Lezinska, Robbie Oniel, Manolis, Harriet Grant, Simon Ford, Tapatheo, Shannon Fischer, Claire Bertin-Lang, Mark Holmes, Karl Franz, Jacob Briars, Ian Mclaren, Sara Denton, Jackie Summers, Alvin Haywood, Sean Johnson, Adrian "Passionfruit" Biggs, John Cicero, Anna Mcloughlin, Erin Stevens, Filthy Daniel, Justin Savage, Caesario De-Medeiros, Dale Degroff, Mark Fairweather, David Catania, Charles Hardwick, Shamila Salvi, Pamela Mostacero, Sullivan Doh, Almir Santos, Julio Cabrera, Chris Cabrera, Ingrid Best, Francesca Hogi, Philip Pepperdine, Gardner Dunn.

When you don't have siblings, you have cousins . . . lots of them. Love y'all. Junior, Tyrone, Sandra, Latonia, Reality, Omar, Lynn, Darnell, Kori, Gemma, Amy, Denise, Karla, Jessica, Troy, Washieka, DJ, Pam, Jason, Tanisha, Marvin, Danette, Tim.

The MadBloggers, OCSupreme and QuaJay (formerly known as Throatchop), for birthing "LadyBlogga" and giving me my first space to exercise my pen.

Pam Pincow (Evins), Sabrina Crider, Amanda Greenfield (Zeno), for trusting me with your spirits brand content and becoming really great friends in the process.

Shane Breen and Levar Thomas, for trusting me with the SD brand for years . . . pre- and post-Complex.

Karlie Hustle, because when life shows me its ass, your words of wisdom Moonstruck-slap me back into reality. Never too much. Always just enough. Appreciate you.

Liz Connelly, watching you grow SEED from the ground up has been an inspiration like no other. For women by women, motivating and inspiring women . . . oh, and kick-ass tacos when it matters.

Thank you, Matt Doyle, for shooting your best shot. And Pearl for overseeing said shots.

Thank you, Louisa Brown-Thank you for your continued love and support.

A Special thanks, Douglas Ankrah- your impact has affected all black mixologists around the world and will be felt for many generations to come. Thank you for your pioneering attitude and unwavering belief in yourself and all the community. You were one of a kind.

Special thanks to the Yellowbrick Crew. Teamwork makes the dream work.

To everyone who has ever supported any of my work, I appreciate you. Thank you.

ACKNOWLEDGEMENTS
COLIN ASARE-APPIAH

Louisa Brown-Thank you for your continued love and support.

William Asare-Appiah, Dimitri Lezinska, Robbie Oniel, Manolis, Harriet Grant, Simon Ford, Tapatheo, Shannon Fischer, Claire Bertin-Lang, Mark Holmes, Karl Franz, Jacob Briars, Ian Mclaren, Sara Denton, Jackie Summers, Alvin Haywood, Sean Johnson, Adrian "Passionfruit" Biggs, John Cicero, Anna Mcloughlin, Erin Stevens, Filthy Daniel, Justin Savage, Caesario De-Medeiros, Dale Degroff, Mark Fairweather, David Catania, Charles Hardwick, Shamila Salvi, Pamela Mostacero, Sullivan Doh, Almir Santos, Julio Cabrera, Chris Cabrera, Ingrid Best, Francesca Hogi, Philip Pepperdine, Gardner Dunn, Gareth Howells.

A Special thanks,

Douglas Ankrah- your impact has affected all black mixologists around the world and will be felt for many generations to come. Thank you for your pioneering attitude and unwavering belief in yourself and all the community. You were one of a kind.

BIBLIOGRAPHY

Bell, Emily. "The Overlooked History of Black Mixology" Vinepair, February 4, 2016 https://vinepair.com/wine-blog/the-all-too-quiet-history-of-black-mixology/

Byck, Daniella. "A New Cocktail Series Honors DC's Black Bartenders, Past and Present" Washingtonian, August 30, 2019. https://www.washingtonian.com/2019/08/30/a-new-cocktail-series-honors-dcs-black-bartenders-past-and-present/

Cohn, Alicia. "Toasting The History Of Drinking In The District" Washington Examiner, May 5, 2013. https://www.washingtonexaminer.com/toasting-the-history-of-drinking-in-the-district

Davis A, Luke. "The Mint Julep and Black Bartenders Who Popularised It" Cultrface, August 8, 2020. https://cultrface.co.uk/mint-julep-black-bartenders/

Djegal, Philippe. "The History Behind Napa Valley's Black-Owned Estate Winery" Kron4, February 25, 2019. https://www.kron4.com/news/the-history-behind-napa-valleys-first-black-owned-estate-winery/

Expert Editorial. "Solutions and Words of Wisdom From Black Female Vineyard Manager, Brenae Royal" Wine Industry Advisor, June 30, 2020. https://wineindustryadvisor.com/2020/06/30/solutions-and-words-of-wisdom-from-black-female-vineyard-manager-brenae-royal

Givens, Dana. "This Man Is Bringing World's First African And Caribbean Rum To The United States." Black Enterprise, June 26, 2020. https://www.blackenterprise.com/this-man-is-bringing-worlds-first-african-and-caribbean-rum-to-the-united-states/

Happy Hour City. "Bar History: Cato Alexander" Happy Hour City, https://www.happyhourcity.com/blog/bar-history/cato-alexander

Hines, Nick. "Why Is Liquor Called 'Spirits' " Vinepair, March 7, 2017. https://vinepair.com/articles/why-liquor-called-spirits/

Kilgore-Marchetti. "New American Whiskey Inspired By Historic Montana Female Bootlegger" Whiskey Watch, June 28, 2019. https://thewhiskeywash.com/whiskey-styles/bourbon/new-american-whiskey-inspired-by-historic-montana-female-bootlegger/

Lux Row Distillers. "Mint Julep Cocktail: A Quick History" LuxRowDistillers, May 2, 2018. https://luxrowdistillers.com/mint-julep-cocktail-history/

Nick, Breaking Bourbon. "The Story of Uncle Nearest 1856 Whiskey" Breaking Bourbon, May 24, 2018. https://www.breakingbourbon.com/article/the-story-of-uncle-nearest-1856-whiskey

Schwarz, Philip. "Dabney, John (ca 1824-1900)" Encyclopedia Virginia, Virginia Humanities. February 12, 2021

Smallwood, Karl. "Where Does The Practice of 'Pouring One Out For Your Homies' Come From" Today I Found Out, December 3, 2018. http://www.todayifoundout.com/index.php/2018/12/where-does-the-practice-of-pouring-one-out-for-your-homies-come-from/

Supercall. "10 Overlooked Stars of Cocktail Culture" Thrillist, February 27, 2017. https://www.thrillist.com/culture/overlooked-stars-of-cocktail-culture

The Three Drinkers. "Uncle Nearest: A True, Black, Whiskey Icon" TheThreeDrinkers, June 3, 2020 https://www.thethreedrinkers.com/magazine-content/uncle-nearest-founding-father-tennessee-whiskey

Walhout, Hannah. "9 Things To Know About the Dark and Stormy History of Rum" Food And Wine, August 8, 2017. https://www.foodandwine.com/cocktails-spirits/rum/brief-history-rum

Wight, Kate. " 'Pouring One Out' Explained: History, Meaning and Getting It Right" Join Cake, January 8, 2020. https://www.joincake.com/blog/pour-one-out/

Wondrich, David. "The Lost African-American Bartenders Who Created the Cocktail" Daily Beast , January 29, 2021. https://www.thedailybeast.com/the-lost-african-american-bartenders-who-created-the-cocktail

Kingston Imperial

Marvis Johnson – Publisher
Joshua Wirth – Designer
Kristin Clifford – Publicist, Finn Partners
Roby Marcondes – Marketing Manager

Contact:
Kingston Imperial
144 North 7th Street #255
Brooklyn, NY 11249
Email: Info@kingstonimperial.com
www.kingstonimperial.com

Photography copyright ©2022 by Madelynne Ross of Bites and Bevs LLC and Kingston Imperial, LLC.
Styling by Proper Garnish LLC.

Kingston Imperial is committed to publishing works of quality and integrity. In that spirit, we are proud to offer this book to our readers; however, the story, the experiences, and the words are the author's alone.

For information address Kingston Imperial, LLC
Rights Department, 144 North 7th Street, #255 Brooklyn N.Y. 11249

Published by Kingston Imperial, LLC
www.kingstonimperial.com

Cataloging in Publication data is on file with the library of Congress

Black Mixcellence: A Comprehensive Guide to Black Mixology by Tamika Hall with Colin Asare-Appiah

Photographs by Madelynne Ross of Bites and Bevs LLC

Design by Joshua Wirth of PixiLL Designs, LLC

Hardcover ISBN: 978-1954220188
Ebook ISBN: 978-1954220195

Printed in China

First Edition

BLACK MIXCELLENCE

A COMPREHENSIVE GUIDE TO BLACK MIXOLOGY